Jack Skeen | Greg Miller | Aaron Hill

THE PURPOSE WORKBOOK

Part of the Circle Blueprint System

Published by:
Griffin Publishing
314 E. Lake Shore Drive
Tower Lakes, IL 60010
Phone: (847) 910-1640

ISBN: 978-0-9993388-3-4

Library of Congress Control Number: 2017956816

Printed in the United States of America

TABLE OF CONTENTS

INTRODUCTION TO PURPOSE

INTRODUCTION TO PURPOSE

The Purpose Workbook offers a system to help you decode the conscious and unconscious factors that affect your success. Purpose is the fourth fundamental development area of *The Circle Blueprint*—which you may have read, but which is not entirely essential. There are also workbooks for the other three fundamental development areas (Independence, Humility, and Power), and you may wish to also work through the other three after you work through the Purpose Workbook to more fully develop your Circle Blueprint. The system in this workbook is intended for anyone with an interest in developing a higher mastery of the element of Purpose. People who develop a mastery of Purpose have a clear understanding of how to deploy the gifts they have in life in the most useful manner.

ASSESSING YOUR PURPOSE

If you have read *The Circle Blueprint*, you are likely familiar with the self-assessment tool available at www.thecircleblueprint.com. This tool, which we will explain below for those who are who are either unfamiliar or who want a reminder, helps you understand where you are on various factors that constitute the element of Purpose. If you are comfortable with the assessment process, you may want to proceed to the After Self-Assessment section.

SIX FACTORS AFFECT OUR ABILITY TO GAIN PURPOSE:

1. **Resolute:** Clearly knowing your destination before your start your journey, thoughtfully determining your progress, and the ability to choose wisely.
2. **Diligence:** Deliberately and persistently acting in pursuit of a goal.
3. **Myopia:** Inflexible, closed-minded thinking.
4. **Experience Sharing:** How we communicate events to others.
5. **Self-Deception:** The act of misleading oneself.
6. **Spirituality:** Seeing that life is much bigger and more complex than what is material.

The Circle Blueprint provides in-depth explanations of these factors, but this overview should give you a gist of it, and the results of your assessment, or even honest self-reflection on these issues, will let you know where you may need further development or better balance.

Specifically, the assessment results provide descriptions on our "Thriving Scale." On each factor, you should have a score.

1. I am ***hanging on*** by my fingernails. Despite all I have accomplished, my life isn't good at all.
2. I am ***eroding***. I'm not desperate but my life is a grind and does not seem to be headed in a positive direction.
3. I am ***treading*** water and just sort of enduring my situation. My life isn't bad, but I would not say it is good, either.
4. I am ***growing***. My life is on a positive trajectory. Certainly, it could be better, but I am reasonably satisfied and optimistic about the future.
5. I am ***thriving***. I am creatively engaged in my work and life. I am at the top of my game. I feel energized, balanced, healthy, and happy.

AFTER SELF-ASSESSMENT

Once you have an idea of where you are on each factor, you can proceed to the exercise series. We have broken these out according to where you fall on the Thriving Scale. In this way, you can go through various exercises according to where you are. That is, if you are hanging on, complete the exercises that align with hanging on, and if you are growing, you can complete the exercises that align with growing. There are no exercises for areas where you are thriving because you do not need further development in those factors. We have included multiple sessions to allow you to work on developing each factor over time. After you complete Session 1, you can move to Session 2 and so on. Further, you can also repeat the assessment or even work on your own development over time—after you complete the "treading water" exercises, for example, you can move onto the "growing" exercises. We have often found it helpful to revisit the exercises at one level of the Thriving Scale a few times if need be, and in other instances, just moving to the next level after one pass may be sufficient. The system is flexible for you and 100 percent self-driven—you complete the exercise series as you see fit, but this offers you a system for developing your Circle Blueprint at your own pace and in total privacy.

EXERCISE SERIES: RESOLUTE

FACTOR – RESOLUTE

This construct describes the trait of clearly knowing your destination before your start your journey, thoughtfully determining your progress, and the ability to choose wisely.

SELF-ASSESSED RATING - HANGING ON

You rarely, if ever, consider the big picture, what you are trying to achieve, or monitor progress toward goals.

SESSION 1

EXERCISE 1A – RESOLUTE, HANGING ON

You are hanging on by your fingernails in your life primarily because you are not resolute. The purpose of these exercises is to enable you to understand what it means to be resolute and to see how your weakness in this area is undermining the effectiveness of your life. You cannot take responsibility to fix your life until you can clearly see the areas that need to be addressed.

Session 1 focuses your attention on the fact that you hardly ever think about the bigger picture in anything you do. You don't consider what you are trying to accomplish when you make decisions and don't relate your choices to any plan or goal. It is almost as if you do whatever comes into your mind whenever that occurs without making connections to anything else.

TASK: Over the next week notice how you make decisions and how rarely, if ever, they are made in the context of a bigger picture.

EXERCISE 2A – RESOLUTE, HANGING ON

Notice that because you don't have the big picture in mind, you rarely, if ever, know if you are making progress in anything you do. There is no goal. There is no plan. So, there is no way to way to even define what it means to be making progress. Your choices are completely independent of one another so they don't lead anywhere. It is no wonder that you aren't making progress in your life.

TASK: To see this clearly in your own life, write down three goals and the progress you have made toward them. If this is difficult, or impossible, it should help you to better understand your situation.

EXERCISE 3A – RESOLUTE, HANGING ON

Observe that you don't make wise choices. One reason it is difficult for you to make wise decisions is that without a clear destination in mind, it is impossible to tell a wise decision from a foolish one. The difference between the two only becomes clear when you know what you are trying to accomplish and what you are trying to avoid. It is a wise decision to limit what you eat if you are trying to lose weight. It is a foolish thing to do if you are starving.

TASK: Make a list of at least 10 decisions you have made in the past few months. Can you define which are wise and which are foolish? If so, how do you know the difference? If not, you can better understand the difficulty you create for yourself when you aren't resolute.

EXERCISE 4A – RESOLUTE, HANGING ON

See that you lack the discipline to stick with a course of action. In some ways, this is an unfair statement. It can be difficult to know if you lack the ability to discipline yourself or not. When you aren't resolute, there is nothing to discipline yourself to do. There is no course you are trying to follow. There is no goal you are trying to achieve. Hence, there is no need for discipline of any sort. Discipline is only of value when you are trying to create something for yourself. You may notice the lack of discipline in your life and wonder why it is so lacking. You may not have fully considered the results that lack of discipline might have on your life.

TASK: In order to see your lack of discipline, compare your life to that of people you know whose life is more successful than is yours. Do you notice that all of them have greater discipline than you?

SESSION 2

EXERCISE 1B – RESOLUTE, HANGING ON

Focus your attention on some of the reasons you may not have learned to be resolute in your life. While there are no valid excuses for not cultivating this trait, noticing why you may have missed it might assist you in closing some necessary gaps in the way you live your life. Let's get started.

Exercise 1 invites you to notice that you might have never learned to be resolute from the people who raised you. If you were raised by people who lack this trait it might be easy for you to undervalue it in your life now.

TASK: Take some time to consider how your parents live with regard to this trait, as well as any siblings you may have. You may notice that it isn't a trait that is widely held in your family.

EXERCISE 2B – RESOLUTE, HANGING ON

Notice if you have so much chaos in your life that being resolute seems like a mountain too high to climb. Being resolute is about creating order. It might seem impossible to create order if you are surrounded by disorder. You might not know where to begin. Like a hoarder who has lived in a mess for years, the idea of cleaning up and removing clutter may seem hopelessly complex. Consider the amount of chaos in your life. You may have chaos in your finances, health, relationships, employment, children, neighborhood, and on and on.

TASK: Make a list of all the areas of your life that seem chaotic.

EXERCISE 3B – RESOLUTE, HANGING ON

Exercise 3 invites you to notice if you lack the self-discipline to be resolute. You may see the value of creating order and purpose in your life, but it seems almost impossible for you to follow any course of action. You are so drawn to whatever appears before you that you bounce between activities for no apparent reason other than the fact that they caught your attention. You may have not yet learned how to say "no" to yourself in order to create something better.

TASK: Assess your ability to discipline yourself by rating from 1 (quite good) to 5 (quite poor). If you lack self-discipline, do you know why? It is important to try to answer this question honestly.

EXERCISE 4B – RESOLUTE, HANGING ON

Consider that you may not see any reason to be resolute. Your life is in disrepair. That is clear. But, you may have never made the connection between not being resolute and the current condition of your situation. You may not know how important purpose is in building a successful and happy life. You may not realize that building a life is like building a house; you must lay one brick at a time. It can be a difficult and tedious project. It isn't always fun, but, the house doesn't get built unless you have determined the height and width of the wall, and have laid every brick in its place. If you aren't resolute, you may either lay the bricks haphazardly, wherever you feel like putting them, or you might find that laying bricks isn't much fun and stop to watch TV. Either way, the wall won't get built. Your life won't get built either until you cultivate this skill. How important do you think it is to be resolute? Be honest with yourself.

TASK: Rate your conviction from 1 (Being resolute is very important) to 5 (Being resolute is not important at all).

SESSION 3

EXERCISE 1C – RESOLUTE, HANGING ON

This session focuses your attention on some of the results that follow from not being resolute. The better you see the connection between this trait and the problems you experience in your life, the more motivated you should be to cultivate it.

Exercise 1 invites you to see that your life has little or no purpose. Purpose is like "true north" for a human being. Without purpose, there is little meaning in life. Nothing much seems to matter. There is little or no motivation to try to accomplish anything.

TASK: Write a paragraph about the meaning of your life. State clearly what is important to you. Write down what you are trying to accomplish. Then, list five ways your life is suffering because you lack purpose.

EXERCISE 2C – RESOLUTE, HANGING ON

Exercise 2 invites you to see your life lacks order. Since you are not resolute, you create no roadmap for your life, nothing to order it. You can't determine what is important to you and what is not. You can't tell what is helpful and what is hurtful. You can't set priorities because you don't know where you are trying to go. Your life is disorganized in a fundamental way.

TASK: Notice the disorder of your life. Make a list of five ways that disorder is obvious to you. Consider things like the cleanliness of your home, your finances, your health, and your friendships.

EXERCISE 3C – RESOLUTE, HANGING ON

Notice that your life isn't progressing. There was a time when you made progress in your life. When you were very small you couldn't even turn over. Then, you learned to turn over. You then learned to crawl, then walk, and then run. There was a time when you couldn't speak. You cried, learned to talk, and then learned to read and write. Your life was progressing on many fronts, but as you grew older, you stopped progressing and stagnated. You lacked the resolute nature to order your life. Then, it began to decay from the lack of forward momentum.

TASK: List five ways you have noticed your life falling into disrepair.

EXERCISE 4C – RESOLUTE, HANGING ON

Exercise 4 encourages you to notice that your life may be in trouble. If your life is decaying, you are headed in a dangerous direction. The mess you have left unattended is likely to only get worse because decay breeds decay. Your lack of order in your life may have cost you your career. Your inability to provide for yourself might cost you your family. The loss of your family may cost you your mental health. The downward spiral is serious and can be deadly. All of this is the result of your lack of being resolute.

TASK: Track the course of your life from its high point to today. If you continue on this path, what is the likely course?

SESSION 4

EXERCISE 1D – RESOLUTE, HANGING ON

Session 4 focuses your attention on some basic things you can do to stop the decline of your life before it is too late. Each of these skills will require change and may take time to master. Let's get started.

Exercise 1 invites you to make your life matter to you. All positive change starts with the commitment to make your life important to you. It is your first and most important commitment in life to care for yourself well. That doesn't mean do whatever feels good. It means it is your job to build a good life for yourself. At this point, you are not demonstrating that commitment. You are letting yourself down.

TASK: Take some time and consider if you are truly willing to make that commitment. If you are, write it down and put it somewhere you will see it every day. It should say something like, "I commit my energy and effort to create the very best life for myself that I can build."

EXERCISE 2D – RESOLUTE, HANGING ON

Put a stake in the ground. Not literally. We mean decide that you will stop allowing your life to decline today. You need to make a clear decision to do things differently than you have in the past. While it may take a while to dig yourself out of the hole you are in, that won't happen until you stop making the hole deeper. The day you make that decision, you will stop doing the things you know are making things worse and will begin doing things that will make your life better. Only you can decide when you are ready to make that decision. It does you no good to try to fool yourself if you aren't ready. But, if you are, make that commitment to yourself.

TASK: Write down, "Today, I take 100 percent responsibility for every choice I make, and I will do my very best each day going forward to build the best possible life I can for myself."

EXERCISE 3D – RESOLUTE, HANGING ON

Pick one issue on which to focus your attention. Change happens one step at a time. It is often a slow process, but speed isn't important. Focus is important. Your life might be messy and in disarray. It won't get put back in shape overnight. But, now that you have put a stake in the ground, pick one issue that you want to work on. It should be something that will make a meaningful difference. It should not be something that is complicated and will take a long time to fix. You might pick something like de-cluttering your home. That might be a big task but it is something you can take on and complete in a day or two. Success breeds success. When you pick even something simple and complete it, you will be encouraged to take on something else.

TASK: Make a list of things you should take on to get your life in order. Then, pick one to focus on.

EXERCISE 4D – RESOLUTE, HANGING ON

Create a goal, make a plan, and stick with it. Now that you have an issue you want to master, you need to prove to yourself that you can be the master of your own life. You do this by setting a goal for that area and then getting there. This is not just a decision; it is a journey. In order to take that journey, you will need to create a roadmap. What needs to happen first? Second? Third? When do you want to have completed the first step? The second? The third?

TASK: Take your time and create a thorough roadmap for the issue you want to address. Include milestones and dates when you want to reach them. Now, get to work.

FACTOR – RESOLUTE

This construct describes the trait of clearly knowing your destination before your start your journey, thoughtfully determining your progress, and the ability to choose wisely.

SELF-ASSESSED RATING - ERODING

You set some goals, but they are vague and you rarely maintain your energy and focus to achieve them.

SESSION 1

EXERCISE 1A – RESOLUTE, ERODING

Your life is eroding, at least partly, because you are not sufficiently resolute. The purpose of these exercises is to help you to understand what it means to be resolute and how your weakness in this trait is contributing to the decline you see in your life. It is also to assist you in developing skills that will make you more resolute and will arrest any further decline in the quality of your life. Session 1 focuses your attention on understanding what it means to be resolute. Let's get started.

Exercise 1 invites you to see that people who are resolute start almost every project they take on by getting clear as to their goal; what they are trying to accomplish. When they eat, they are considering the impact of the calories on their weight and of the nutrition on their health. They have decided how healthy they want to be. Those who aren't very resolute rarely consider the big picture. They tend to make decisions without considering what they are trying to accomplish or the impact of those decisions on their lives.

TASK: Rate yourself from 1 (You always start with getting clear as to what you are trying to accomplish) to 5 (You never start with getting clear as to what you are trying to accomplish).

EXERCISE 2A – RESOLUTE, ERODING

Exercise 2 invites you to see that people who are resolute thoughtfully measure their progress toward their predetermined goal. If they determine they want to have a certain amount of money in the bank before they retire, they create a savings plan that they regularly monitor to ensure it remains on track. Those who are not so resolute either set no goals, or set goals but don't check to see how they are progressing toward them. The result is either a sense of aimlessness to their lives, or a series of goals that never go anywhere. Your life doesn't seem to be making any progress. Because you are not effectively directing it, it is slowly sliding toward chaos and problems that are overwhelming.

TASK: Rate your habit of measuring progress in your life goals from 1 (I do this regularly) to 5 (I never do this at all).

EXERCISE 3A – RESOLUTE, ERODING

See that people who are resolute choose wisely. Life is filled with decisions. You make hundreds of decisions every day. You decide when you will get up, what you will wear, what you will eat for breakfast, and how you will get to work. The list goes on and on. Those who are resolute know every decision they make is either helpful or hurtful in advancing their goals. Hence, they are thoughtful and disciplined in making each one. Those who are not so resolute don't operate as if there is much connection between their choices and their goals (if they have them). Instead, they make their decisions based on whatever they want in that moment. The result is that their decisions are random and don't lead anywhere. They are more based on impulse than on thoughtfulness.

TASK: Rate yourself in how wisely you make choices from 1 (very thoughtfully and wisely) to 5 (no thought or wisdom at all).

EXERCISE 4A – RESOLUTE, ERODING

Exercise 4 invites you to see that people who are resolute stick to their course. Reaching goals requires a certain amount of self-discipline. You must be able to stay focused on your destination over a lengthy period of time and to say no to all that tempts you to divert from that path. Those who are resolute are skilled at self-discipline. Reaching their goals is highly motivating to them, and is so important that they resist being distracted. Those who are not so resolute have little or no self-discipline. They may be well-intended when they set a course or establish a goal, but other interests easily distract them and they quickly forget about the commitments they made to themselves and others. The result is that few goals ever are reached.

TASK: Rate your ability to discipline yourself from 1 (very self-disciplined) to 5 (no self-discipline).

SESSION 2

EXERCISE 1B – RESOLUTE, ERODING

Session 2 focuses your attention on ways you see the value of being resolute play out in the lives of others and the benefits they receive for having cultivated this trait. Often, seeing the choices others make will make it easier to see how you can change your life.

Exercise 1 invites you to see that your friends who are more resolute than are you have more order in their lives than do you. They just seem more organized, as if they have a plan for almost everything. Your life feels more chaotic and scattered. You might see many examples of order. They may have regular routines as to how they spend their time. They might make purchases guided by a budget. They might have certain rituals as a family, such as the time they eat meals and bedtime routines that are absent from your life.

TASK: Pick a family or two that seem to be more resolute than are you, and list five illustrations of order in their lives that your life is lacking.

EXERCISE 2B – RESOLUTE, ERODING

Notice that those who are more resolute than are you seem to create more progress in their lives than do you. If you have known these people for a long time, you can clearly see that they seem to be headed somewhere. Perhaps they moved from their starter house to one big enough for their family, while you feel stuck in your starter home. Or, they may have the money to go on vacations that you can't afford. They didn't always have the success they now enjoy. They have moved toward it steadily and patiently, while your life has declined.

TASK: Pick a family or two that seem to be more resolute than are you and list five ways you have seen them progress.

EXERCISE 3B – RESOLUTE, ERODING

Notice that those who are more resolute than are you have many more disciplines that you have in your family. They have rules that guide them in almost all they do. They have rules about how much television the children are allowed to watch, how much candy they can eat, and the time they go to bed. The parents have rules about what they will spend money on and how much they will save. They have rules about the kinds of things they will say to each other and words they won't use. You don't have many rules. You sometimes seem to be all over the map about how you do things.

TASK: Pick a family or two that seem to be more resolute than are you, and list five rules you notice they have but you don't.

EXERCISE 4B – RESOLUTE, ERODING

Observe that those who are more resolute than are you have workability to their lives that your life lacks. Their lives are getting stronger. It is working. It keeps getting better. It is almost as if they keep figuring things out better and better as the years go by. Things just seem to be working out for them. Their children are doing well at school. Their careers seem to be progressing. They seem happier and more successful than are you and your family. Their attention to being resolute is paying off in tangible and undeniable ways.

TASK: Pick a family or two that seem to be more resolute than are you and list five ways you see that their lives are more workable than is yours.

SESSION 3

EXERCISE 1C – RESOLUTE, ERODING

Session 3 focuses your attention on some of the ways your life is suffering because you aren't sufficiently resolute. This is like looking in the mirror. You might not always like what you see, but you need to see it if you are going to fix it. Some soul-searching can be very helpful in prompting change.

Exercise 1 invites you to notice that your life is in disorder. You might not have noticed this until you started these exercises, because you acclimated to the disarray in your life. But, now that you have looked at some of your more successful friends, you are beginning to admit to yourself that you have a fair amount of chaos in your life. Perhaps you have very few routines. You might never have mealtimes, and everyone just fends for him- or herself. You might not have bedtimes, and people are sleeping wherever and whenever they please. You might not organize your money, and so have no idea what you can and can't afford.

TASK: List 10 ways your life is disorderly.

EXERCISE 2C – RESOLUTE, ERODING

Exercise 2 invites you to notice that there is a sloppiness to the way you live. It isn't that you are just disorderly; you are also wasteful. Because things aren't well organized, you find yourself wasting time and money. You need to buy things repeatedly, because you have no place where you keep them, and so you misplace and lose them. You don't plan meals, so food spoils and goes to waste. You don't organize your time, so you end up wasting time, procrastinating, or just using time inefficiently. Over time, such waste accumulates and leads to sloppiness.

TASK: List 10 ways you could describe your life as sloppy.

EXERCISE 3C – RESOLUTE, ERODING

Notice that your life is suffering a decline that, while slow, is progressive and dangerous. Just as you noticed that your friends' lives seem to be on a positive trajectory, you now are beginning to notice that yours is on a negative one. Their lives are getting stronger, but yours is getting weaker. While their children seem to be thriving, yours have habits that are beginning to undermine their success socially and at school. Your neglect of various aspects of your life is starting to show up in financial pressure that doesn't seem to have a clear solution, and a sense that things aren't good and seem to be getting worse, rather than better. This sense of decline is important to face. It is not likely to reverse on its own. It is only by cultivating the trait of being resolute that you will be able to turn it around.

TASK: List five ways you know your life is declining, and where it is likely to be in three years if you don't turn it around.

EXERCISE 4C – RESOLUTE, ERODING

Recognize if there exists a sense of hopelessness, that might be creeping into your thinking because you don't know what to do to make your situation better. You can feel your life sliding in the wrong direction. You know this is happening because you have allowed your life to exist in such a weakened state. Hopelessness can actually be helpful when it motivates you to action. But, there is also a temptation to ignore it because it feels so big.

TASK: Notice the hopelessness you are beginning to feel and see if you can write it down. Write whatever comes to mind. Don't hold back and don't shy away. This exercise might be the very thing that prepares to you to make the changes that need to be made.

SESSION 4

EXERCISE 1D – RESOLUTE, ERODING

Session 4 focuses your attention on some fundamental changes you can make that will stop the decline of your life so you can begin to rebuild. All of them are focused on aspects of being more resolute in how you deal with your life.

Exercise 1 invites you to envision a brighter future. The current state of your life is not nearly as important as your ability to envision what you want it to be; what it can be. If you can see it, you can build it. If you can't see it, it is almost impossible to build.

TASK: Use what you learned about the lives of those who are currently experiencing more success than you to construct a picture of the life you want to have. Feel free to borrow the pieces of their lives that are attractive. Be clear and concrete. The first practice of being resolute is getting clear about what you want to commit to. Once you have completed that list, review it each day for the next week, focusing on making it so important to you that you won't rest until you have achieved everything on the list.

EXERCISE 2D – RESOLUTE, ERODING

Make a plan. It isn't enough to make a list of what you want. You must now make a plan of how you will get there from where you are now. You must have a plan. It doesn't have to be complicated, but it must include clear steps that you can follow. If your goal is to have enough money to buy a new house, determine how much money that is, when you want to have it, and how much money you will save each month to get there. Your plan is necessary because it will help you to stay focused on your progress. You will be able to see if you are moving in the right direction. You will also see when you are beginning to stray off course. In this way, it will assist you in being resolute toward your goal.

TASK: Pick one goal and write a plan.

EXERCISE 3D – RESOLUTE, ERODING

Remember to take one day at a time. It can be daunting to take on a plan that will take years to complete, but if you focus only on what you need to execute today, it seems much more manageable. Today you will make decisions that either move you toward the fulfillment of your plan, or further from it. Begin to pay attention to your decisions in light of your plan. This will support the discipline you need to get where you want to go. It will make it more difficult for you to be impulsive. Practice being thoughtful before making your decisions, weighing the impact of each choice on your plan.

TASK: Consider the longer term impact of your choices. After you have given it some thought, make the wise choice. Keep a record of the decisions you have made and evaluate that list every day to determine if you made the wise choice.

EXERCISE 4D – RESOLUTE, ERODING

Enlist support in being resolute. When you endeavor to change habits, it can be quite helpful to have the support of some trusted friends. They can review your goals, plans, and decisions and give you feedback as to how you can make them clearer and more compelling. They can encourage you when you are tempted to stray from your plan, reminding you of the benefits of being resolute. They can get you back on track when you quit.

TASK: Make a list of five people who care about you and whom you can trust to support you in your growth. Meet with each one and tell them what you are doing. Check in with them at least once each week until you can reliably stick with your plans.

FACTOR – RESOLUTE

This construct describes the trait of clearly knowing your destination before your start your journey, thoughtfully determining your progress, and the ability to choose wisely.

SELF-ASSESSED RATING - TREADING WATER

You set goals and progressively achieve them, but they tend to be focused on stability rather than expansion.

SESSION 1

EXERCISE 1A – RESOLUTE, TREADING WATER

You are treading water, at least partly, because you are sufficiently resolute to maintain the life you have created, but not enough to move toward growing and expanding your life. These exercises are designed to assist you in understanding how the quality of being resolute contributes to the goodness you are experiencing, and why it is important for you to expand this quality in order to improve. Session 1 focuses your attention on what it means to be resolute in your life. Let's get started.

Exercise 1 invites you to see that those who are resolute never engage in any project before they have decided precisely what they intend to accomplish, and why that is important to them. In other words, they have goals for all of the aspects of their lives and don't make themselves content with the current state of affairs. Those who are less resolute are playing more of a defensive game. They know they don't want the life they currently have, but they don't have a lot of drive or ambition to do more.

TASK: Rate your level of being resolute from 1 (great ambition) to 5 (content with how things are).

EXERCISE 2A – RESOLUTE, TREADING WATER

See that those who are resolute are very thoughtful as to how they will achieve their goals. In other words, they create order in every area of their lives. They understand that they won't achieve their goals unless they have meaningful, logical, and thorough plans that outline the steps to get there. The orderliness of their lives is obvious. It seems that everything they do has its place in their plan. Those who are not so resolute may not be sloppy in how they live, but they order only those parts of their lives that are necessary to maintain what they have, and to keep things from eroding. For example, they might have a plan to manage their money so they can pay all of their bills on time, but they might not have a sufficient plan for retirement, or for a major change, like buying a new house. There may be pockets of their life where they lack much, or any, order.

TASK: Rate your level of being resolute from 1 (You order everything) to 5 (You have pockets of your life that lack order, and/or you don't have order for advancing your life).

EXERCISE 3A – RESOLUTE, TREADING WATER

Those who are resolute are mindful in every decision they make. They are keenly aware that there are no small decisions. Every decision either advances their goals or undermines them. While they might have whims and impulses, they are run through the filter of careful thought before a decision is made. Their decision-making has seriousness to it. Those who are less resolute are aware that many decisions are important, and need to be made wisely and thoughtfully. But, they have other areas of their lives where they aren't so careful, and might act impulsively and with little thought. They aren't likely to spend the money they need for the mortgage, but might go on a shopping spree with their extra money without considering if that extra cash could have been used in a more productive way.

TASK: Rate your level of being resolute from 1 (thoughtful about every decision) to 5 (quite impulsive in decision-making).

EXERCISE 4A – RESOLUTE, TREADING WATER

Observe that those who are resolute are disciplined in everything they do. They know that success will largely be determined by how consistently they stay on track with their plans and goals. They know that deviating from the plan only makes things more difficult. Every wasted action or decision means they will have to work harder and longer to get where they want to go. Hence, they don't often deviate from their plans, and when they do it is not by very much. Those who are less resolute have some areas where they are disciplined, but also some where they are not. They might discipline themselves at work so they can advance their career according to their plans, but drink too much at night without much thought to the wasted time and the consequence to their health.

TASK: Pick one or two people you know who seem to be more resolute than you. List three habits you observe that supports their ability to stick with things that move them toward their goals and keep them on track. Then, see if you find evidence in your life of those same habits.

SESSION 2

EXERCISE 1B – RESOLUTE, TREADING WATER

Session 2 focuses your attention on how being resolute has been helpful to you. The more clearly you see the benefit this trait brings to your life, the more you will be encouraged to make it even stronger. Let's get started.

Exercise 1 invites you to see how resolute you are in building the success you have in your life. It isn't an accident that you are doing as well as you are. You imagined it a long time ago. You had dreams for your success that have directed and guided your actions for many years. It is often a good idea to think back to earlier years and to recall your dreams. You probably had in mind the kind of home you wanted to have, the neighborhood you wanted to live in, the amount of money you wanted to make, and the size family you wanted to have. Your commitment to those dreams was a critical piece to creating them.

TASK: Make a list of some of the dreams you had long ago and then note how many of them have been fulfilled.

EXERCISE 2B – RESOLUTE, TREADING WATER

Exercise 2 invites you to see how resolute you have been in steadily and diligently progressing toward your goals until they were reached. You had a plan that you stuck with regardless of what was going on around you. This isn't easy. It is easy to become distracted and forget the direction you determined to go. It is easy to become discouraged when things are difficult and aren't going as you expected. But, you disciplined yourself to stay on track and to keep moving forward. Your discipline has been instrumental in your success. Moreover, discipline is like a muscle; the more you exercise it, the stronger it gets.

TASK: Take a few moments and list some of the ways you see your discipline showing up in your life. Then list some of the ways you see it has contributed to your success.

EXERCISE 3B – RESOLUTE, TREADING WATER

Exercise 3 invites you to see how resolute you have been in tracking your progress. You know that some goals take a long time to accomplish and are best broken into smaller, more bite-sized pieces. You have done this with almost all of your goals. You had a view of your career success, but knew it would require progressing through a number of different jobs in order to acquire the skills and experience you needed. It may have required numerous employer changes as well. But, through it all, you were focused on obtaining what you needed in order to move to the next rung on the ladder. You set your sights on the next step, took it, enjoyed seeing your progress, and then refocused on the next one. Your progression has been steady and consistent.

TASK: List three goals and the progress you made to reach them.

EXERCISE 4B – RESOLUTE, TREADING WATER

Exercise 4 invites you to see how resolute you have been in making thoughtful and wise decisions. You know the goodness of your life has been built one brick at a time. You have made thousands of decisions, each one either advancing toward your goals or slowing your progress down. You considered each one against your dream, chose wisely, and acted courageously. It was this resolute focus on selecting the right decision that allowed you to be in good health, get the right education and training, save for your home, and build the right friendships. You have done a very good job of choosing wisely.

TASK: Look back over the many choices you have made and make a list of at least 10 very wise choices. Then note the consequences of having picked well.

SESSION 3

EXERCISE 1C – RESOLUTE, TREADING WATER

Session 3 focuses your attention on ways you may not yet be sufficiently resolute to move beyond treating water. When you notice how limitations in being resolute are limiting your success, you may be motivated to make changes that will strengthen this attribute. Let's get started.

Exercise 1 invites you to notice that while you seemed quite resolute to build the life you have got, you don't seem to be so resolute about taking it to a new level. You may have grown content with your level of success. You may have already surpassed the quality of life you expected to have. But, without having dreams for your future around which you are highly committed, it isn't likely that you will move beyond treading water.

TASK: See if you can list five dreams you have to expand or improve your life. Then, rate your commitment to each from 1 (highly committed) to 5 (not committed).

EXERCISE 2C – RESOLUTE, TREADING WATER

Exercise 2 invites you to notice your choices. While it is certainly true that you are quite careful to make wise choices in many areas of your life, there are some where you might have little or no discipline. You might manage your money well, but waste a fair amount of time. Or, you might keep your house neat but eat way too much of the wrong stuff. Your lack of being resolute over all of your choices is limiting your ability to advance your life. You are accepting being okay rather than pressing forward to having the very best life you could have.

TASK: List five areas where you know you don't make wise and careful choices.

EXERCISE 3C – RESOLUTE, TREADING WATER

Exercise 3 invites you to notice the limits to being resolute around your progress. There was a time when you were highly motivated and focused. You were determined to reach your goals, and you kept track of your progress as a way to stay focused and feed your discipline. But, now that you have reached many of your goals, you have less passion and commitment. Instead, you can see some laziness in how you conduct yourself. Your life may not be sliding backward, but it isn't moving forward. Perhaps it is holding steady. Unless you increase being resolute, it isn't likely that your life will progress much beyond where it is now.

TASK: List five ways you can see that you aren't demonstrating much discipline to make your life better.

EXERCISE 4C – RESOLUTE, TREADING WATER

Exercise 4 invites you to notice that your attitude has become one of resignation more than passion. Being resolute requires a fierce determination; one filled with energy, drive, and power. You may recall times in the past when you had a great deal of motivation and drive. But, you may notice now that you have less of both. Perhaps you are fearful of losing what you have built in the quest for more. Or, perhaps you are unclear as to what you want next. Regardless, until you reconnect with your passion and inner fire, you aren't likely to move to the next level. Notice your passion for change.

TASK: List some times in the past when your passion was higher. Note some signs of your resignation.

SESSION 4

EXERCISE 1D – RESOLUTE, TREADING WATER

Session 4 focuses your attention on concrete changes you can make to become more resolute in the development of your life. Clearly, things aren't bad. But, they could be better. The key to getting there is focusing on these changes. Let's get started.

Exercise 1 invites you to shift your attention from your current level of satisfaction to seeing your potential. You should be delighted that your life is stable and relatively secure. But, you may not be asking yourself the right question. Perhaps you should consider if you are living up to all of your potential. Do you have the ability to function at a higher level at work? Could you gain skills that would change your role? Can you relate to people on a higher plane? If so, perhaps you should continue to press on. You don't have to. But, part of the satisfaction in life is from taking on new challenges and pressing on to the next opportunity.

TASK: Do an assessment of your potential as a person. Does it seem to you that you could do more? If so, in what areas of your life could you do more?

EXERCISE 2D – RESOLUTE, TREADING WATER

Exercise 2 encourages you to get excited about the possibilities. Being resolute requires your excitement and passion. It is very difficult to drag yourself into change. It is much easier when you are excited about what you are doing and where you are going. Excitement grows as you see the benefits you will gain from completing the journey you are about to undertake. You could become excited about the next things you will learn, or the opportunity to do things that are different and that will require more of your creativity. You might become excited about the expanded success you will have, and the opportunities for travel and adventure that you will be able to afford.

TASK: Make a list of at least five benefits you will receive from moving forward in your life.

EXERCISE 3D – RESOLUTE, TREADING WATER

Exercise 3 invites you to commit. Commitment is a big deal. Half-hearted commitments aren't commitments at all. It is only when you are all in, that you are sufficiently resolute to do what needs to be done to make things happen. In the previous exercises you considered some changes you could make to your life. And, you focused on the benefits from achieving those changes such that you should have some excitement about the possibilities. Now, you must ask yourself if you are ready to commit. Notice if, when you ask yourself that question, you have any hesitancy. If so, pay attention to it. Until it is gone, you aren't quite ready. Perhaps you are a bit frightened of what will be required of you. That is okay. Perhaps you should be a bit scared.

TASK: Return to your list of benefits, and remind yourself of all that you are planning to get from the change. Revisit your decision about commitment until you are fully committed.

EXERCISE 4D – RESOLUTE, TREADING WATER

Exercise 4 invites you to stay the course. Assuming you committed to some change, you must now be resolute in your conviction to stick with the change until you have reached the end. The worst thing you can do to yourself is to commit to a change and then not complete it. Doing so can hurt you more than if you hadn't begun to change. You commit to school and pay the tuition, but lose interest and stop going to class. Now you have lost the tuition money and have nothing to show for it. Staying the course requires repeatedly reminding yourself of the benefits you are planning to get, noting your progress, and disciplining yourself when you are tempted to stray or to quit.

TASK: Practice with something short term and small. It could be saving money for something you want to buy. The more you practice being resolute, the better you will become at it.

FACTOR – RESOLUTE

This construct describes the trait of clearly knowing your destination before your start your journey, thoughtfully determining your progress, and the ability to choose wisely.

SELF-ASSESSED RATING - GROWING

You have a big vision of who you can be and where your life can go and, for the most part, set clear goals and make steady progress toward them.

SESSION 1

EXERCISE 1A – RESOLUTE, GROWING

You are growing in your life, at least partly, because you have largely mastered the quality of being resolute. However, you aren't yet thriving. There may be some places where you have not been willing to be resolute, or you may have a few sacred cows that you have continued to hold on to, even though they are limiting your growth. The goal of these exercises is to help you understand what it means to be resolute, see how being resolute has helped you to grow, identify where you may need to grow in this trait, and then give you some help in expanding your ability to be resolute. Session 1 focuses your attention on exactly what it means for you to be resolute. Let's get started.

Exercise 1 invites you to see that you have been resolute in your belief that your life can continually get better and better. You certainly would not have allowed your life to fall into disrepair. Moreover, despite your success you were not willing to become complacent and lazy. You have been resolutely committed to the idea that you always want to be growing and evolving. Pay attention to how resolute you have been in your commitment to a better life.

TASK: Make a list of the times when you have evolved your life over the years. Note that it is still in the process of evolving.

EXERCISE 2A – RESOLUTE, GROWING

Exercise 2 invites you to see how resolute you have been in patiently and persistently moving forward to your goals. You, like everyone, encountered obstacles and difficulties along the way. Your life hasn't always been easy, but you did not allow difficulty to be an excuse to stop moving forward or to settle for less than you could have. It may have slowed you down from time to time, but you kept moving forward and kept your eyes on your goal. This persistence to keep progressing despite adversity and difficulty has served you well.

TASK: Note five times when you persisted in persevering, even when things were difficult and discouraging.

EXERCISE 3A – RESOLUTE, GROWING

Exercise 3 invites you to see how resolute you have been in making wise choices. It is no accident that your life is growing. Almost every decision you make is chosen because it fits your plan for your life. You are thoughtful about every decision because you know that a wrong one has the power to derail your plans, and a right one can make a powerful contribution. You always knew you wanted to be a lawyer, so you carefully picked the law school you wanted to attend, because graduating from that school would set you up for a powerful career. You researched their admissions standards, and then carefully chose the right classes and extracurricular activities that would appeal to their admissions board. You knew the classes you had to ace, and you chose to study with extra diligence in those classes. You crafted your life one choice at a time.

TASK: Make a list of five choices that were wise, deliberate, and helped shape your life.

EXERCISE 4A – RESOLUTE, GROWING

Exercise 4 invites you to see how resolute you have been in your self-discipline throughout your life. You haven't allowed yourself to be diverted from the responsibility of making your life special. There certainly have been many opportunities for you to do other things, or to be distracted by the interests of others. But, you have stayed the course, avoiding distractions and keeping yourself focused on your goal; to have the best life you could have. Your resolute commitment has served you well, and your self-discipline has only grown over time. You can see that your discipline and consistency have been necessary to get where you are. Take some time to appreciate the discipline you have shown in cultivating your life.

TASK: Make a list of five temptations you have resisted, and the benefit you received from having done so.

SESSION 2

EXERCISE 1B – RESOLUTE, GROWING

Session 2 focuses your attention on how you have benefitted from being resolute. It is so valuable to see the benefits of this trait in your life. Let's get started.

Exercise 1 invites you to see how important being resolute is in your growth as a person. While it might not be true that being resolute creates expansion in your life, it is certainly true that to the extent you lack being resolute, expansion will not be possible. Growth is difficult. It requires learning new things, taking on new challenges, and overcoming obstacles. These things are not done without courage, tenacity, and persistence. Only those who are resolute will continue to push forward when things are difficult. As you look at your life, you can notice that you have never stopped expanding. Your life has been a continual progression of changes; giving up the comfort of your current life in order to reach for more. You have not stopped and this pattern is now part of your how you operate.

TASK: Make a list of the challenges you have faced and overcome. Now, add those challenges you are facing and pushing through. Take a few moments to appreciate being resolute in supporting your expansion.

EXERCISE 2B – RESOLUTE, GROWING

Exercise 2 invites to you to focus on all you have learned as a result of being resolute. You have learned a great deal because your life has continuously expanded, exposing you to new ideas, environments, cultures, and challenges. You have also learned a great deal from being resolute. You have learned to focus, to weigh the consequences of your choices, to curb your impulses, and to build self-discipline. In fact, this trait has been a good teacher, one who has strengthened your wisdom and character.

TASK: Take a few moments to notice how you have seasoned and matured as a person, as a result of being resolute. List five lessons you have learned.

EXERCISE 3B – RESOLUTE, GROWING

Exercise 3 invites you to see how being resolute has made you successful. Much, if not all that you have is the result of your persistence. You were resolute in your parenting, keeping your eye on the prize of raising your children to be well equipped for their lives. So, you were patient, dependable, wise, constructive, and generous to them even when they tested your patience. Now, you enjoy your success as you see their lives blossom. You were resolute in the pursuit of your career and put in the long hours, applied yourself to mastering your craft, and kept raising your hand for new opportunities. The result of your perseverance is evident in your professional reputation and in the wealth you have produced for yourself and your family.

TASK: Make a list of the major ways you are wealthy, and notice the role being resolute has played in your success.

EXERCISE 4B – RESOLUTE, GROWING

Exercise 4 invites you to see how being resolute has contributed to your happiness. There is a price to be paid for being resolute. You may not have always been the most spontaneous person. You may have not impulsively bought that sports car that caught your eye just because you wanted it. No, you were thoughtful, deliberate, and careful. But, being resolute has rewarded you with happiness that is more stable and secure than the short-lived thrill of impulsiveness.

Your life feels strong, secure, solid, and good because you have been resolute in building it that way. Now, you look around you and feel good about all you have done. You did it the right way.

TASK: Make a list of five ways you experience happiness because of your life success. See if you can connect these things to being resolute.

SESSION 3

EXERCISE 1C – RESOLUTE, GROWING

It is great that you are growing, but you aren't yet thriving. It is possible that there are some gaps or unresolved issues that limit your commitment to being adequately resolute to get your life to the next level. Session 3 focuses your attention on four possibilities, and invites you to see if any of these are holding you back. Let's get started.

Exercise 1 invites you to notice if there are any people in your life with whom you are unwilling to be resolute. You might be quite skilled at disciplining yourself in most of your life, but there is someone who you are unwilling to deal with as directly as necessary in order to thrive. You might have a soft spot for your children and aren't willing to be as disciplined as you need to be to support the development of the life you want them to have. Or you might be afraid of upsetting your spouse, so you hold back on part of your plan for your life. Or you could be unwilling to be as direct as you need to be with your boss, and so aren't advancing at work as fast as you planned.

TASK: Make a list of people you might not be willing to deal with directly, and so are not being as resolute as you need to be for your life.

EXERCISE 2C – RESOLUTE, GROWING

Exercise 2 invites you to notice if you have some indulgences that you are unwilling to get under control even though they undermine your life; even if in some small way. People have all kinds of pet indulgences. For some, it is their temper. They are quite controlled in every other, way but they occasionally snap at people. For others, it is some habit like drinking, watching television, or gambling. They are quite disciplined in every other way but not in this one thing.

TASK: Review your life and make a list of any habits you hold onto and which you, up until now, have been unwilling to tame by being more resolute.

EXERCISE 3C – RESOLUTE, GROWING

Exercise 3 invites you to notice if you are facing any obstacles that you are unwilling to take on. You have been growing and expanding, taking on one challenge after another, but now you find yourself facing something that has stopped you in your tracks. For some reason, it seems bigger and more difficult than things you have faced before. You don't seem to be resolute enough to push into it and fight through it. You may have advanced your career, but this next step is a big one. It might require uprooting your family and moving across the country. This seems so big and disruptive, you have balked at even thinking about it, let alone facing it.

TASK: Make a list of any challenges that are stopping you from progressing. Write down what seems difficult about these particular challenges.

EXERCISE 4C – RESOLUTE, GROWING

Exercise 4 invites you to see if you have some laziness that is undermining your characteristic commitment to being resolute. You have been growing and pushing forward your whole life. In some ways, it is natural to hit a plateau and to think that this is good enough. This is a good enough job. My children are in a good enough place. My marriage is good enough. But, that kind of thinking will entice you to stop being resolutely committed to being all that you can be. It is certainly okay to rest after you have accomplished some goal you have set out to do, but then it might be time to sign up for the next challenge.

TASK: Take a look at your life. Are you resting or have you grown complacent and lazy? Are you ready to sign up for something new?

SESSION 4

EXERCISE 1D – RESOLUTE, GROWING

Session 4 focuses your attention on some ways you can become even more resolute, so as to move from growing to thriving in your life. Let's get started.

Exercise 1 invites you to get very clear about what you want. It is easy to have a general idea of your hopes for the future. It is not as easy to become definite in every detail of your life as to what you want to create. The clearer you get, the more you can be resolute to build it. The fuzzier you are, the less resolute you are likely to be. Getting clear is a test of your conviction. If you aren't clear, you may not be very committed to making that thing happen in your life. You may have a vague idea that you want to take a vacation next year. That is very different from knowing you want to hike the Grand Canyon from rim to rim in September next year.

TASK: Review your life, and see if there are areas where you aren't that clear about what you want. Spend some time thinking about those areas, and see if you can write down a statement that captures exactly what you want to create.

EXERCISE 2D – RESOLUTE, GROWING

Exercise 2 invites you to assess the challenges you will face if you take on creating those things you outlined in Exercise 1. You got clear about some goals that are important to you, but you have not yet taken them on. Perhaps you have been avoiding getting clear because you had a sense they would require taking on some big challenges. Now that you have become clearer, you can see the obstacles better. It isn't wise to set out to make any change until you have calculated the price you will have to pay, and decided if you have the resources to afford it. Growth in any area will require an investment in time, energy, money, and focus. You have limited resources. What will you have to sacrifice in other areas of your life to expand in the one you are contemplating? Is this the best time to take on a new challenge? If not, when is a better time? What preparation do you need to make? These are important questions to answer.

TASK: Take one change you are thinking of making, and list the challenges you will face when you take it on.

EXERCISE 3D – RESOLUTE, GROWING

Exercise 3 invites you to consider who you will need to be in order to move to the next level. You have a way of being in your life right now. You have habits, routines, indulgences, and disciplines that allow you to effectively function. When you change and move to the next level in your life, you will need to make changes in many of these things. It is almost as if you will need to choose to be a different person. This can be a very positive and useful exercise. You may be able to be quite effective now, but if you are going to take on the next level of your fitness you will need to lose 20 pounds. First, you need to take on a commitment to being that kind of an athlete. Once you have committed to being that person, you will develop the routines, disciplines, and attitudes that support the person you have decided to become.

TASK: Write down who you will need to be to move to the next level of your life.

EXERCISE 4D – RESOLUTE, GROWING

Exercise 4 invites you to put that new person into play. Once you have decided who you need to be to function at that next level, start today to be that person. If today you are going to move your parenting to the next level, think of yourself as an outstanding parent and begin to act like one. Pay more attention to your children. Be less concerned about yourself. Spend more time thinking about their future. Set aside time when you will speak with them one on one. Whatever change you want to make in your life requires consistently acting like the person you want to be. Be resolute in your commitment to be that person.

TASK: Write down what you will do each day this week to be the person you are now committed to being.

EXERCISE SERIES: DILIGENCE

FACTOR – DILIGENCE

Taking care of your own affairs, remaining calm under pressure, and avoiding impulsive behavior are all important in acting with deliberateness. Diligence requires the ability to pay attention to important details, and to follow through on successive tasks that advance your goals.

SELF-ASSESSED RATING - HANGING ON

You have almost no ability to stick with your goals and plans.

SESSION 1

EXERCISE 1A – DILIGENCE, HANGING ON

You are hanging on by your fingernails, at least partly, because you have little or no diligence in how you conduct your life affairs. These exercises are designed to help you understand the concept of diligence, see where it is lacking in your life, understand the consequences of its absence, and then take a first step toward becoming diligent. Session 1 focuses your attention on four aspects of diligence so you begin to understand the concept. Let's get started.

Exercise 1 invites you to see that the foundation of diligence is taking care of your own affairs. Those who are diligent understand their life is their responsibility. They believe it is up to them to do all they can do to build a successful life. On the other hand, those who lack diligence are expecting others to take care of them. They either don't think it is their job to manage their life, or don't think they are up to the task.

TASK: Rate your diligence in terms of taking care of your own affairs from 1 (You take full responsibility) to 5 (You don't take any responsibility).

EXERCISE 2A – DILIGENCE, HANGING ON

Exercise 2 invites you to see that those who are diligent remain calm under pressure. They know that building a good life is a long-term process that doesn't happen overnight. They know there will be problems to solve and setbacks to overcome along the way. Hence, when misfortune arrives, they take it in stride. It is just another thing to deal with. Those who lack diligence freak out when things go bad. They become completely unglued and are either stopped in their tracks or frantically active but unproductive. It seems that almost any pressure is too much for them to deal with.

TASK: Rate your level of diligence in terms of your ability to deal with pressure from 1 (calm under pressure) to 5 (unable to handle pressure).

EXERCISE 3A – DILIGENCE, HANGING ON

Exercise 3 invites you to see that those who are diligent are thoughtful, planful, and careful in their behavior. They are following a plan. They know what they are trying to do. They have thought about the life they want to have and how they will build it, and the steps are being carefully followed. Those who lack diligence don't seem to have a plan. They make decisions largely on impulse. They do whatever comes to mind in the moment. As a result, it is difficult to make sense of their choices. You can't easily see where they are headed, or if they are making progress. The course of their life is erratic and a bit chaotic.

TASK: Rate your level of diligence as it relates to being planful from 1 (Decisions are thoughtful and planful) to 5 (Decisions are impulsive).

EXERCISE 4A – DILIGENCE, HANGING ON

Exercise 4 invites you to see that those who are diligent follow through on their commitments and agreements. They make commitments to themselves to do what they believe is important. They make agreements to others. They know that keeping their word is critical to success. If they commit to stopping smoking, they quit. If they aren't ready to quit, they don't commit. If they tell their boss they will have the report on his desk by Friday at noon, it is on his desk at that time. Those who aren't diligent either don't make commitments and agreements, or they break them easily and often. Their word doesn't mean that much to them. They easily make excuses for themselves. The result is that they rarely stick with a course of action to the very end.

TASK: Rate your level of diligence in terms of following through on your commitments and agreements from 1 (always follow through) to 5 (almost never follow through).

SESSION 2

EXERCISE 1B – DILIGENCE, HANGING ON

Session 2 focuses your attention on how you experience the lack of diligence in your life. The more clearly you see its absence, the better you will understand its need. Let's get started.

Exercise 1 invites you to see the sense of helplessness you broadcast to the world around you. You have come to believe that your life is too much for you to deal with by yourself. Having come to that conclusion, you have abdicated responsibility to build a successful life. Now, you are like a shipwrecked sailor holding on to a piece of driftwood floating in the ocean, hoping for favorable winds and tides or some boat to come along. This sense of helplessness undermines any determination to take control because you see it as impossible. This helpless attitude undermines any positive change.

TASK: Over the next three days, make a list of every time you think or act as if you are helpless in building a good life for yourself.

EXERCISE 2B – DILIGENCE, HANGING ON

Exercise 2 invites you to see that you are almost completely reactive in how you live your life. You don't have a plan for any part of your life. You never think about a better future and how you will build it. Instead, you wait to see what the day will present and then react with whatever comes to mind. Because you don't have a bigger picture view of your life, your decisions don't move you in any direction or build anything solid. You are like a leaf in a stream, being carried along without any destination or ability to steer a course.

TASK: Over the next three days, notice how you are reactive. Make a list of five times when you acted without giving thought to a bigger picture or plan.

EXERCISE 3B – DILIGENCE, HANGING ON

Exercise 3 invites you to see that you are impulsive about almost every decision. Instead of asking yourself if something makes sense, you make decisions based on whatever emotion rises to the surface. If something makes you happy or creates a good feeling, you are quite likely to do it. If it gives you a bad feeling, you are likely to pass on it. But, your feelings have little connection with what is best for you. It might feel good to take drugs but doing so might ruin your career and your life. Impulsive decisions are fine when the consequences are minimal. Your lack of thoughtful planning makes it impossible to know when a decision has major consequences and when it has very minor ones.

TASK: Over the next three days, keep a list of the impulsive decisions you make.

EXERCISE 4B – DILIGENCE, HANGING ON

Exercise 4 invites you to see that you are scattered in how you live your life. Your thinking is scattered. It isn't focused. You bounce from topic to topic. You start and then stop things. You have an abundance of unfinished projects. You have not created a pattern of starting something and following it through to the very end before you start something else. You sometimes feel quite overwhelmed because you have so many loose ends that haven't been tied up. The more you feel overwhelmed, the harder it is to get motivated to do anything. Hence, it is easy to quit trying and procrastinate some more.

TASK: Over the next three days, make a list of unfinished projects and times when you procrastinate because you feel overwhelmed.

SESSION 3

EXERCISE 1C – DILIGENCE, HANGING ON

Session 3 focuses your attention on how the lack of diligence is negatively affecting your life. You may have a better understanding of how you experience a lack of diligence, but it is also important that you gain a better understanding of the price you are paying for its absence. Let's get started.

Exercise 1 invites you to see that you are viewed by others as someone who needs to be cared for, rather than as someone who has something to offer. This is a huge distinction. When the people around you see how you live your life, they might feel sorry for you and feel some obligation to help you. But, they don't see you as someone who might bring value to their lives. They don't see you as someone they would want to employ or embrace as a friend. The best you have done is to create the kind of relationship where you might receive a handout or some temporary assistance. This is terribly unfortunate, because until you demonstrate value and utility, your life won't progress.

TASK: Take some time to do an assessment of how you are viewed by your friends. List the ones who think you bring some value to them, and the value they see. Next, make a list of those who see you as someone who needs their assistance. Which list is longer?

EXERCISE 2C – DILIGENCE, HANGING ON

Exercise 2 invites you to see that your life is viewed as chaotic and woefully disorganized. You stand out as the person who doesn't have her act together. Your lawn is overgrown, your yard filled with abandoned toys, your house in disrepair, your clothes unkempt, your children undisciplined, and your work record erratic. It is as if you haven't been able to get your act together in any area of your life. You are seen as someone whose life is in danger of collapse. You may have grown accustomed to living as you do and may not realize how poorly your life is viewed by those around you.

TASK: Take a walk around your house and make a list of things that are in need of repair. Don't quit until you have finished listing everything.

EXERCISE 3C – DILIGENCE, HANGING ON

Exercise 3 invites you to see that you are seen as someone who can't take feedback or criticism. People are careful around you because they don't want to set you off. They know that any comment, even meant to be helpful, can be taken by you as if it is a criticism. Any criticism can devastate you, throwing you into depression and withdrawal. As a result, no one is willing to tell you what you need to hear. Everyone colludes with you in avoiding confronting the mess you are making of your life.

TASK: Over the next three days, notice how rarely people will say anything negative to you. Even if you ask for criticism, people won't give it for fear of hurting you.

EXERCISE 4C – DILIGENCE, HANGING ON

Exercise 4 invites you to see that you are making no progress whatsoever in your life. Without diligence, it is almost impossible to make life better. Because you lack the ability to effectively follow through on any effective plan, your life has stagnated. When you look over your shoulder, you might see that nothing has changed over the years except that you have gotten older, and unfortunately, unless your life is getting better, it is probably getting worse. Life supplies a natural flow of challenges that must be mastered in order to move ahead. If they aren't mastered, those same challenges will begin to exert a drag that pulls you toward chaos.

TASK: Make an honest assessment of your life, and make a list of at least five ways that you notice progressive decay.

SESSION 4

EXERCISE 1D – DILIGENCE, HANGING ON

Session 4 focuses your attention on some clear and concrete steps you can take to build resolve in your life. Keep in mind that you are starting from the beginning. But, building some strong, basic habits can have a real and lasting effect in your life. Let's get started.

Exercise 1 invites you to value order over chaos in your life. You must come to see that the way you are living isn't sustainable. You must look around and see that your friends and family who create order in their lives have a much better quality of life than do you. Simply acknowledging the value of order is the first step toward diligence. See if you are ready to take it.

TASK: As you look at your life, do you see the need to change? Does the chaos and disorder seem like a problem for you? Be honest with yourself.

EXERCISE 2D – DILIGENCE, HANGING ON

Exercise 2 invites you mentally organize your life. It might seem overwhelming to create order in your chaotic life, but the first step is to get mentally organized. See if you can picture your life with less chaos. What would that look like? How would things be different? Start with your physical setting. What would it look like for your house to be neat? What things that are broken would be fixed? What has been neglected that would be tended to? Imagine your yard neat and mowed, you house organized, your time allocated according to priorities.

TASK: Take some time to make a list of how your life would work if it was organized and planful.

EXERCISE 3D – DILIGENCE, HANGING ON

Exercise 3 invites you to put a stake in the ground. No one can tackle everything at once. Instead, diligence starts with narrowing your focus to one issue you will take on. And, it is important to pick the right one. The right one is often one where you see a clear start and a clear finish, one that won't take a long time to complete, one where you have all you need to complete it, and one you can start soon. An example might be mowing the lawn. You have neglected the lawn for a long time, but it will only take about an hour to mow, you have a mower and gasoline, and you have time to do it today. If all that is true, mowing the lawn might be a good stake in the ground. You can determine that you will take it on today, and you will finish it today. Then, you can sit outside and admire the results of being diligent. You took control of one part of your life, even a small one, and created order for the moment.

TASK: Review all that needs to be done to get your life in order, and pick one thing that will be your stake in the ground.

EXERCISE 4D – DILIGENCE, HANGING ON

Exercise 4 invites you to keep going. Your stake in the ground was a good beginning, but this could be a long journey. The first step gets you moving in the right direction and now you must order the next few steps. Take out your list of things that need to be ordered. You did a good job picking the best one to be your stake in the ground. Now, pick the next best one to take on. It should fit the criteria we used before. It should have an obvious beginning and ending. You should have all the resources you need to complete it, and you should be able to start it now. Once you have identified it, pick the next one. Once you have picked the next three, go back and actually do the first one. This is the pattern of diligence.

TASK: Once you start being diligent, keep moving forward.

FACTOR – DILIGENCE

Taking care of your own affairs, remaining calm under pressure, and avoiding impulsive behavior are all important in acting with deliberateness. Diligence requires the ability to pay attention to important details, and to follow through on successive tasks that advance your goals.

SELF-ASSESSED RATING - ERODING

You are quite easily distracted or discouraged from sticking with your goals and plans.

SESSION 1

EXERCISE 1A – DILIGENCE, ERODING

Your life is eroding, at least partly, because you lack sufficient diligence to create stability and security. These exercises are designed to help you to better understand diligence, to see how diligence has helped you, how your weakness in this area is undermining your success, and to help you expand your diligence. Session 1 focuses your attention on better understanding the concept of diligence. The better you understand it, the more easily you will recognize where you have it and where it is lacking. Let's get started.

Exercise 1 invites you to see that diligence is the ability to take care of your own affairs. When you are diligent, you demonstrate ownership of your life. You know it is your responsibility to manage every aspect of your career, your family life, your friendships, your personal habits, and your home. Ownership is such an important concept. You have pride in your ability to manage your life well. When you lack diligence, you treat your life more like you are a renter. It is not your job to keep your life in good repair. That responsibility belongs to someone else.

TASK: Rate your diligence in terms of how much ownership you have over all aspects of your life from 1 (100 percent ownership) to 5 (not much ownership at all).

EXERCISE 2A – DILIGENCE, ERODING

Exercise 2 invites you to see that diligence is the ability to remain calm in the midst of stress and pressure. Growth requires change. Change is almost always stressful because it requires learning new things, adapting to new challenges, and giving up old ways of thinking and acting. The only way to avoid the stress of growth is to make the choice to avoid it. You lack diligence if you have a low tolerance for stress. Instead of accepting stress as part of the process of having an effective life, those who are low on diligence do everything they can to minimize or avoid stress. They simplify their lives as much as possible. They avoid challenges. They pass up new opportunities. But, avoiding stress comes at the price of failing to build a more effective life. Eventually, you realize you aren't keeping up and instead are starting to slide backwards.

TASK: Rate your diligence in terms of how much you are willing to accept stress into your life from 1 (very accepting of stress) to 5 (avoiding stress as much as is possible).

EXERCISE 3A – DILIGENCE, ERODING

Exercise 3 invites you to see that diligence is the ability to act deliberately. Those who are deliberate are thoughtful and planful in what they do. They have a master plan for their life and understand that their every action has an impact, either positive or negative, on that plan. Hence, they think through the implications of their choices before they act, and then discipline themselves to act in ways that strengthen their life. Those who are not as deliberate may not have a master plan at all. They may not think about the implications of their decisions on the quality of their life. Or, they might consider it but lack the discipline to do that which would be best for themselves. They seem a bit impulsive.

TASK: Rate your level of diligence in terms of your deliberateness from 1 (very thoughtful in making decisions) to 5 (hardly ever considering the implications of your decisions on your life).

EXERCISE 4A – DILIGENCE, ERODING

Exercise 4 invites you to see that diligence is the ability to stick with your plans regardless of what is going on in your life. There is steadfastness to those who are diligent, and the ability to keep their eye on the target no matter what is happening. That steadfastness comes from the clarity of mind that the goal won't be reached without consistency and steady process. Those who aren't so diligent have difficulty sticking with their plans. They might have competing plans that vie for their attention. Or, they may be easily distracted by things that capture their attention in the moment. Regardless, they are easily blown off course. As a result, it is difficult for them to make steady progress.

TASK: Rate your level of diligence in terms of your ability to be steadfast in pursuing your goals from 1 (quite steadfast) to 5 (not steadfast in the least).

SESSION 2

EXERCISE 1B – DILIGENCE, ERODING

Session 2 focuses your attention on how you might see diligence showing up in the lives of people you know. You can learn a great deal from people who seem to be more successful than you currently are. When you see how they are benefitting from being diligent, you can apply those same principles in your life. Let's get started.

Exercise 1 invites you to see that your more successful friends and neighbors demonstrate planfulness in their lives. It is almost as if they have a blueprint for the life they want to have. The car they drive fits their budget and their circumstance. It is neither too big, too small, too expensive to operate, nor too expensive to buy. It fits them perfectly. Their home fits their family. If they have a child, they have enough room to be together and to be apart. They might have a yard in which to play. They live in a neighborhood selected for its good school. As you look at their lives, you may see that you don't have a plan like theirs.

TASK: Pick someone you know who is more successful than you. List five ways you can see that they have a plan.

EXERCISE 2B – DILIGENCE, ERODING

Exercise 2 invites you to see that your more successful friends have an order for how they do things. They have routines that make sense. They mow the lawn on Saturday morning, go to the park on Sunday afternoon, eat dinner together at 6:00 every evening, and the kids are in bed regularly at 8:30. The order in their lives suggests stability, as if each of these routines was chosen for a reason. Dinner gives them time to connect as a family. Bedtimes give the parents a much needed break. Mowing the lawn keeps their yard neat and clean. You don't have nearly as many routines as do they. You might say to yourself that routines are too restrictive, but you might be making yourself feel better by being unwilling to acknowledge the benefit they bring.

TASK: Pick a family that seems to have their act together a bit better than does yours, and list five routines they have that your family does not.

EXERCISE 3B – DILIGENCE, ERODING

Exercise 3 invites you to see that your more successful friends seem to have a discipline in their lives that is constant and steady. You know them well enough to know that from time to time, they think about taking that big vacation to Europe or buying that new Tesla. They talk about things like that, but they don't act on those thoughts. They are pretty good at saying no to themselves and each other when their desires stray from their plans. It is almost as if they so value their family budget that they are unwilling to make a decision that would mess it up. They would rather postpone a desire or deny it altogether than interfere with the plan they have for their life. Certainly, they have had crises, like when their car broke down and needed a transmission, but because they plan and are disciplined, they had an emergency fund that covered the repairs.

TASK: Pick a family that is more successful than yours, and list five ways you see that they are disciplined.

EXERCISE 4B – DILIGENCE, ERODING

Exercise 4 invites you to see that your more successful friends have big dreams for their lives. When you come to know these folks well, you will discover they have all kinds of things they want for themselves and for each other. They want their kids to be successful adults. They want to retire with enough money to live at the beach. They want to be healthy in their old age. They want to be in love with each other when the kids leave home. You may not have realized that it is precisely these wonderful dreams that motivate them to be diligent. They know that such goals are not easy to reach. Only by charting the course to reach them and sticking with it will those dreams come true. They keep these goals front of mind to help them stay the course and not be tempted to stray.

TASK: Pick one family that is more successful than is yours, and see if you can list five of their big dreams.

SESSION 3

EXERCISE 1C – DILIGENCE, ERODING

Session 3 focuses your attention on your life and how too little diligence might be undermining your success. It is so important for you to connect the dots between this very important trait and the reasons your life is declining. Let's get started.

Exercise 1 invites you to see that you have more wishes that dreams. You want good things for your life, but you haven't gotten clear as to exactly what they are. You have a vague idea that you want to have a good life, but you haven't expended the effort to define what that means to you. Without clarity it is very difficult, if not impossible, to marshal energy and resources to build it. You may not have realized that you lacked clarity until now.

TASK: List five of your more important dreams. Write whatever comes to mind. Then step back and see how specific and clear they are. If they are vague and difficult to measure, they need some work.

EXERCISE 2C – DILIGENCE, ERODING

Exercise 2 invites you to notice that your have few plans as to how you will make your dreams come true. You may not have known how important having a plan was. Or, you may have plans that aren't easy to follow because they aren't clear, or the steps are too big. Clear plans feed diligence, because they break down your big dreams into small steps that can be focused on and attained. Small successes lead to bigger ones, and every success feeds determination.

TASK: Look at your list of dreams. Write down your plans to bring them to life. Step back and see if your plans are easy or difficult to understand and to follow. If they aren't clear and easy to follow, you have some work to do.

EXERCISE 3C – DILIGENCE, ERODING

Exercise 3 invites you to see that you have few routines and rituals. You may say that you value your freedom and like to be spontaneous, but have not realized the value of routines and rituals. Routines dramatically reduce the number of decisions you need to make, because those decisions are part of the routine. If the kids go to bed every night at 8:30, you don't need to decide what time to put the kids to bed every night. Everyone knows it is 8:30. The kids don't fight with you because they know it won't work. You can count on some time for yourself after 8:30. All of this happens because the family has routines. There is order and peace.

TASK: Make a list of the rituals and routines you have in your life.

EXERCISE 4C – DILIGENCE, ERODING

Exercise 4 invites you to see that you don't always handle stress well. Unexpected events can trigger a pretty big reaction, and it is almost always negative. You don't like surprises because they require you to be resourceful and disrupt the status quo. As a result, almost anything new or different can throw you and the family into chaos. People get angry, they yell and scream, and soon any semblance of peace and order is gone. Your emotional reaction to stress disrupts whatever plans or routine you had established. It is almost impossible for the family to consistently and steadily move toward its goals when the high emotionality in the family creates so much upset and distraction.

TASK: List five times in the last week when you and/or your family was thrown into chaos by some unexpected stress.

SESSION 4

EXERCISE 1D – DILIGENCE, ERODING

Session 4 focuses your attention on some specific things you can do to enhance your diligence. Now that you see the need for diligence, it should be easier to address the things that will encourage it to grow. Let's get started.

Exercise 1 invites you to create some big, clear, and exciting dreams for your life and for your family.

TASK: Start with yourself. What do you want your life to look like in five years? Ten years? Don't hold back. Write whatever comes to mind. Don't be practical, but make sure whatever you write down really matters to you. Then, go back and make each dream as clear, measurable, and specific as possible. The clearer you are the better. Finally, review your list of dreams every day for the next week, making tweaks where necessary, until you feel excitement and commitment to making those dreams come true.

EXERCISE 2D – DILIGENCE, ERODING

Exercise 2 invites you to create clear, useful, and detailed plans for how you can reach each of your goals. It is so difficult to consistently move toward big goals, unless you have defined smaller goals that move you toward the fulfillment of your dreams. If you were to sign up to lose 40 pounds, it would be almost impossible not to become discouraged, disheartened, and to give up. But, if you set a goal of losing five pounds each month for the next eight months, you will have a much better chance of being successful. Even better, you could break down your five pound goal into actions you will take today. If you choose to count your calories each day, exercise for certain length of time each day, and weigh yourself once each week, you are much more likely to succeed in losing 40 pounds. Diligence responds best to small goals that can be reached each day.

TASK: So, take one of your goals and create a detailed plan. Make it as easy to follow as you can.

EXERCISE 3D – DILIGENCE, ERODING

Session 3 invites you to create routines and rituals that support movement toward the goals you want to reach. Routines are so helpful because, once they are in place, they reduce the need to make decisions that could undermine your conviction. If you want to lose 40 pounds, you are now going to follow your plan to lose five pounds each month by counting your daily caloric intake and exercising 30 minutes each day. Rituals could include eating the same low caloric breakfast each day at 7:00 a.m. and going to the gym at 5:30 every evening. Once you have done these things for a few weeks, you won't find it nearly as difficult to keep these habits up because you become used to doing them. Your self-discipline is supported by your rituals.

TASK: Make a list of routines and rituals that will support your plans toward your goals. Review your rituals to see if you can make them clearer and easier to follow. Now, put them into play.

EXERCISE 4D – DILIGENCE, ERODING

Exercise 4 invites you to develop the habit of celebrating successes. It is difficult for everyone to stick with their plans, and to avoid distractions and temptations to stray. One of the ways you support and encourage your diligence to stay the course is to celebrate small successes. Celebrations don't need to be extravagant, but they should be frequent enough to keep your enthusiasm high to stay focused. At the end of the month when you have lost five pounds, you should celebrate your success. You might pick one meal and eat whatever you want. Rewarding your success makes it easier to sign up for another month of counting your calories and going to the gym.

TASK: Make a list of some celebrations you can plan when you succeed in reaching some of the goals in your plan.

FACTOR – DILIGENCE

Taking care of your own affairs, remaining calm under pressure, and avoiding impulsive behavior are all important in acting with deliberateness. Diligence requires the ability to pay attention to important details, and to follow through on successive tasks that advance your goals.

SELF-ASSESSED RATING - TREADING WATER

You stick with your goals and plans much of the time, especially those you consider important.

SESSION 1

EXERCISE 1A – DILIGENCE, TREADING WATER

You are treading water in your life, at least partly, because you lack the diligence to move forward. It is not that your life is bad. It isn't sliding backward and falling into disrepair, but it is stagnating. Growing requires more diligence than does maintaining what you have. These exercises are designed to help you better understand the concept of diligence, then see where diligence is working in your life, where it could be better, and how you can strengthen it. Session 1 focuses your attention on better understanding the concept of diligence. Let's get started.

Exercise 1 invites you to see that those who are highly diligent live with a clear sense that there is more they want from their life. They aren't content. That doesn't mean they are discontent either. They are on a path, but haven't reached their destination. Hence, they demonstrate a big commitment to keep moving forward, to keep changing and growing. Those who are not as diligent look around them and have a sense that they have arrived. They may be more successful than they imagined they would be. Regardless, they don't have clarity as to what more they want for their lives.

TASK: Rate your level of diligence, with regard to having clarity as to what more you want from your life, from 1 (You see clearly what more you want) to 5 (You are quite content with the life you have).

EXERCISE 2A – DILIGENCE, TREADING WATER

Exercise 2 invites you to see that those who are diligent demonstrate a determined resolve to face challenges. They know that growth and change don't come without a price. You must be willing to let go of what is comfortable in order to reach for that which is new. You must move into unfamiliar territory and face the possibility you will fall short or fail. You must be willing to learn new things and to try new ways of relating to your world. Hence, they are always making changes in their lives; some big and some small. Those who are less diligent don't change nearly as much. You get a sense that they like things as they are, and enjoy a level of comfort with things staying the same. They don't seem too interested in new opportunities, especially ones that require a lot of effort or a reasonable possibility of failure.

TASK: Rate your level of diligence, with regard to demonstrating resolve to face challenges, from 1 (highly motivated to take on new challenges) to 5 (quite content with things as they are).

EXERCISE 3A – DILIGENCE, TREADING WATER

Exercise 3 invites you to see that those who are diligent possess a steady calm in their demeanor. Not much seems to ruffle or unglue them. It is almost as if they have grown used to facing challenges and difficulty, and so accept them without becoming emotional and upset. Certainly, unexpected problems arise for them, as they do for everyone, but they take them in stride. They seem prepared for difficulty. Those who are less diligent can become quite distressed when problems arise. They hope and expect things to continue to be relatively easy. They aren't emotionally prepared for problems. When unexpected crises arise, they don't handle things well. Rather than stepping into the issue and resolving it as best they can, they become less rational and make choices that don't help to solve the problem.

TASK: Rate your level of diligence, with regard to possessing a steady calm, from 1 (You are quite calm in facing unexpected problems) to 5 (You fall apart when you face crises).

EXERCISE 4A – DILIGENCE, TREADING WATER

Exercise 4 invites you to see that those who are diligent demonstrate a well-seasoned discipline in all they do. Not only do they have a goal and a plan for almost every area of their life, they consistently follow those plans. There is seriousness to how they make decisions. They have taught themselves that it is critical to not deviate from the plan they established for their life, and won't let anything cause them to deviate from that plan. They rarely, if ever, succumb to the temptation to blow off the plan to splurge on something that doesn't advance them toward their goals. Those who are less diligent have more difficulty following through on their intentions. Because they are relatively content with where they are, they are less careful with their resources and are willing to indulge in expenditures of time and money that don't necessarily make life better in any meaningful way. They are more impulsive and indulgent.

TASK: Rate your level of diligence, with regard to being disciplined to stay on course from 1 (highly disciplined) to 5 (not disciplined at all).

SESSION 2

EXERCISE 1B – DILIGENCE, TREADING WATER

Session 2 focuses your attention on where diligence is working in your life. You would not be as successful as you are if you lacked diligence. Seeing it in your life can help you identify ways you can make it stronger. Let's get started.

Exercise 1 invites you to notice that you do a good job of taking care of your affairs. You had dreams for your life and set about making them come true. You haven't expected things to happen on their own. Instead, you took charge of your life and worked hard to build the life you have. It is no accident that you are as successful as you are. You built your life one step at a time until you had it where you wanted it. Your ownership of your life project has served you well.

TASK: Make a list of five areas of your life where you feel successful, and notice how you carefully achieved each one of them.

EXERCISE 2B – DILIGENCE, TREADING WATER

Exercise 2 invites you to notice how you stuck with your plans even when you were tempted to stray. Certainly, there have been times when you grew weary of sticking with your agenda. There may have been things you wanted to buy or do that you chose to bypass because you knew you needed to manage your time and money to reach your goals. You knew diligence was required if you were to get where you wanted to go. It is because you were disciplined and diligent that you finished school, that you progressed in your career, that you had the money to buy a house. It is important to both see and to celebrate your commitment to stay the course.

TASK: Make a list of at least five examples of times when your discipline was necessary for you to achieve your goals.

EXERCISE 3B – DILIGENCE, TREADING WATER

Exercise 3 invites you to see how well you have managed stress. You did not get where you are by taking the easiest path. Your success required taking on some challenges that were difficult and demanding. You had to let go of things that were easy and comfortable in order to gain new skills, have new experiences, and master new challenges. At times, you might have wondered if you would be able to succeed. There may have been times when you were frightened, but you did not let those obstacles and challenges deter you from continuing to move forward. You demonstrated a commitment to reach your goals, even when it was hard.

TASK: Make a list of five times when you faced challenges or discouragement but did not quit.

EXERCISE 4B – DILIGENCE, TREADING WATER

Exercise 4 invites you to see that you have learned how to be calm in a crisis. In the process of persistently and steadily moving forward in your life, you learned to manage your emotions. You couldn't afford to come unglued when bad things happened. Even when you were scared, you mastered the skill of taking a deep breath, assessing the situation, determining your options, and picking the best one. That ability to be calm in the storm allowed you to deal with crises in the best possible manner.

TASK: Make a list of crises you faced. Try to recall the initial feeling you had, and then how you mastered your anxiety and kept yourself calm.

SESSION 3

EXERCISE 1C – DILIGENCE, TREADING WATER

Session 3 focuses your attention on ways limitations in your diligence may be holding you back from moving beyond treading water. The more clearly you can connect your lack of progress with the need for greater diligence, the more motivated you should be to develop that quality. Let's get started.

Exercise 1 invites you to see that you have grown comfortable with your current level of success, and are not taking ownership for further development of your life. It is important that you notice this without shaming yourself. It is not wrong for you to be content, but you might also realize that you do have more potential than you are currently using. You might notice that you used to be ambitious while now you are not. You used to be more adventuresome than you are now. You used to have more willingness to change, and now have become more set in your ways.

TASK: See if you can list five ways you can see that you have become content with the life you now have.

EXERCISE 2C – DILIGENCE, TREADING WATER

Exercise 2 invites you to notice that you lack sufficient diligence to get yourself to do what is required to get to the next level in your life. You certainly have taken on challenges to get where you are today, but you may see that getting to the next level isn't going to be easy. In fact, it will require some changes that you simply aren't willing to make at this point. For example, you might like the idea of running a marathon, but when you checked out the amount of time you would need to invest in training for the event, you gave up on the idea. You just aren't willing or able to discipline yourself to put that many hours into running. In fact, you might see that you don't seem to have the ability to discipline yourself at all beyond what is necessary to maintain what you have.

TASK: See if you can list five ways your self-discipline is not currently adequate to get you to the next level in your life.

EXERCISE 3C – DILIGENCE, TREADING WATER

Exercise 3 invites you to notice that you lack sufficient attention to detail to move to the next level in your life. You are organized enough to keep your life together, but functioning at a higher level would require much greater focus and organization than you are currently demonstrating. The next level at work is far more exacting than your current position. The consequence of making a mistake is much higher. You aren't certain that you are willing to be that disciplined and orderly. You would need to sign up for a more disciplined and diligent style of living.

TASK: See if you can list five ways you would need to pay greater attention to detail if you were to move to the next level of your life.

EXERCISE 4C – DILIGENCE, TREADING WATER

Exercise 4 invites you to notice that you indulge yourself in ways that prevent you from moving beyond treading water. While you manage your money, you certainly don't live by a strict budget. Or, if you have a budget, you don't always follow it. Or, if you follow it, your budget included things you really don't need. You like to give into your whims and wishes, and are not willing to give up that freedom in order to organize your life more than it is currently organized. If you look around, you will notice things you have purchased that you don't use and don't need.

TASK: Make a list of at least five ways you have indulged yourself that don't contribute to a more successful and meaningful life.

SESSION 4

EXERCISE 1D – DILIGENCE, TREADING WATER

Session 4 focuses your attention on changes you can make to strengthen your diligence and so move out of treading water and into growing your life. Let's get started.

Exercise 1 invites you to look for something more than you want for your life. Your life is good...but it could be better. You are relatively successful...but you could be more so. You may be settling for good instead of reaching for more. Until you see something that you don't have and want, it isn't likely you have much of a need to become more diligent. So, let's look for what more you might want. There are a few productive places to look. One is at the lives of others you know who are more successful than are you. Do you want to live in a neighborhood like theirs? Do you want to be in shape like the trainer at the gym? Do you want to have your boss's job or run your own company? Second, look at your potential. What could you do that you aren't doing now? What abilities and gifts do you have that aren't being fully expressed?

TASK: Make a list of anything you want that you don't have.

EXERCISE 2D – DILIGENCE, TREADING WATER

Exercise 2 invites to you increase your desire to get what you want. Diligence is required when you want something you don't have. Until you are highly motivated to go after some goal, you won't begin to exercise and expand your diligence muscle.

TASK: It is often wise to look at the list you created in Exercise 1 and to pick just one thing that you might want to add to your life. Don't pick the hardest. Pick the one that interests you the most. Once you have made your choice, imagine successfully reaching that goal. Consider how it will feel, and how much better your life will be. Use your imagination to be as clear and detailed as you can. Then, make a list of some of the things you will need to do that you aren't doing to reach that goal. Make another list of things you will have to give up in order to reach it. Then, ask yourself if you want to reach this goal enough to actually make these changes. If you aren't willing to make the necessary changes, face it and pick another one. If you are, you have found an issue that should motivate you to be more diligent.

EXERCISE 3D – DILIGENCE, TREADING WATER

Exercise 3 invites you to practice giving things up. You may have difficulty adding new things to your life without first giving something up. If you are going to make time to take classes, you will have to create time in your schedule to go to class. What are you doing now that you are willing to give up? Practicing giving up things for other things, is a great way to expand your diligence. You are doing these exercises. What could you be doing instead of this? What are you giving up to complete these exercises? Everything in life is a trade off. Hopefully, you have discovered a goal that you care enough to attain, that you are willing to make the necessary changes to reach it.

TASK: Make a list of at least five things you are willing to give up in order to reach that goal.

EXERCISE 4D – DILIGENCE, TREADING WATER

Exercise 4 invites you to practice taking things on. It certainly isn't enough to give things up. In order to reach your goal, you will have to do things that you aren't doing now. Some of them will be new and unfamiliar. Others may be challenging and difficult. It is helpful for you to understand what you are getting yourself into so you can emotionally prepare to move forward.

TASK: If you picked a goal you want to reach, lay out the things you will need to do in order to get there. List as many as you can. Review your list and consider each one. Does anything on that list seem too difficult for you to master? Can you see that if you apply yourself to each one, one at a time, you will be able to steadily progress until you have reached your goal? Such forward thinking and planning strengthens your ability to be diligent.

FACTOR – DILIGENCE

Taking care of your own affairs, remaining calm under pressure, and avoiding impulsive behavior are all important in acting with deliberateness. Diligence requires the ability to pay attention to important details and to follow through on successive tasks that advance your goals.

SELF-ASSESSED RATING - GROWING

You stick with your goals and plans even when you encounter difficulty or are enticed by other things, except on rare occasions.

SESSION 1

EXERCISE 1A – DILIGENCE, GROWING

You are growing, as least partly, because you have cultivated diligence in your life. The purpose of these exercises is to help you to better understand the concept of diligence, to see how it has contributed to your success, to help you to identify any lapses in your diligence, and then provide suggestions as to how you can close those gaps. Session 1 focuses your attention on understanding the key aspects of diligence. Let's get started.

Exercise 1 invites you to see that diligence requires clarity of thought and understanding of your potential. The more clearly you can see who you truly are, the life you can have, and your true meaning and purpose, the more determined you will be to create it. To the extent you are unclear, you are more likely to settle for less than you can have. Insecurity and any sense of inadequacy can undermine your diligence.

TASK: Rate your diligence, with regard to how well you know your potential from 1 (very well) to 5 (not well at all).

EXERCISE 2A – DILIGENCE, GROWING

Exercise 2 invites you to see that the diligence needed to move from growing to thriving requires deliberateness in all that you do. There is not much room for wasted energy or resources if you are growing toward fulfilling your potential. You know that time is the most limited resource and that you must make the most of every moment. You understand that any deviation from your course of action will only make it more difficult to reach your goals. You have a single mindedness in your life that many other people lack. While you have free time from work, there is no free time from pursuing your course. Every aspect of your life is ordered and planned with thought and a clear connection to fulfilling your potential.

TASK: Rate your diligence in terms of your deliberateness in every aspect of your life from 1 (deliberate in everything) to 5 (only deliberate in a few areas of life).

EXERCISE 3A – DILIGENCE, GROWING

Exercise 3 invites you to see that diligence requires an emotional steadiness regardless of circumstances. It is not possible to deliberately and consistently move toward fulfilling your goals without having discipline over your emotions. You know that your emotions can be tremendously helpful in staying your course if you manage them well, and you know that if you don't, they can be extremely distracting. You can't afford to be sidelined by fits of anger, or temptations of self-indulgence. You have trained your emotions to key off of your consistent movement toward your goals. You emotionally reward yourself with a sense of well-earned satisfaction for having stayed on track and made progress each day. You are prepared for distractions and label them as such. You have a steady calm in how you carry yourself.

TASK: Rate your diligence, in terms of your emotional steadiness, from 1 (steady through everything) to 5 (steady only in some things).

EXERCISE 4A – DILIGENCE, GROWING

Exercise 4 invites you to see that diligence requires 100 percent ownership of your life. You don't expect others to bail you out or provide you with assistance, even though you are willing to accept assistance when offered. You shoulder the responsibility to fulfilling your potential regardless of what others do or don't do. You never blame others for their choices but you do hold yourself to a very high standard. When things don't work out, you seek to understand your role in the failure, and the lesson you can extract to avoid making the same mistake again. When you succeed, you take it as a learning experience and mentally record every lesson so as to become wiser and smarter. You don't make excuses in any circumstance, accepting responsibility for mistakes. This sense of ownership is what makes diligence work. Because you know you, and only you, are responsible to reach your goals, you take the project very seriously.

TASK: Rate your diligence, in terms of taking ownership of your life, from 1 (You take 100 percent ownership) to 5 (You take only partial ownership).

SESSION 2

EXERCISE 1B – DILIGENCE, GROWING

Session 2 focuses your attention on ways diligence has contributed to your success. Seeing the role diligence has played will help you understand why it is necessary to develop it further. Let's get started.

Exercise 1 invites you to see how committed you have been to continual growth. You have not been willing to accept things as they are, but have kept pressing for more. This commitment to keep developing and improving your life is perhaps the foundation for everything you have. When you look at your friends and those you grew up with, you might see that many of them settled for a certain degree of success in their careers or personal lives. You have not. You diligently dreamed for more.

TASK: Make a list of five dreams that you have found most useful in your life.

EXERCISE 2B – DILIGENCE, GROWING

Exercise 2 invites you to see the role diligence has played in your focus. You have developed, for the most part, the capacity to stay focused on those activities that move your life forward, even when you faced obstacles and problems. This ability to stay on course has served you well. While you saw your friends' lives stall because they lacked sufficient diligence, yours has moved ahead. You keep adding the next step to your successful journey and have no intention of ever stopping. Take some time to notice your diligence and appreciate the role it has played in your success.

TASK: List five incidences when your diligence played a critical role in overcoming a difficult situation and creating a new level of success for your life.

EXERCISE 3B – DILIGENCE, GROWING

Exercise 3 invites you to see the role diligence has played in your self-discipline. Growing is not always easy. Everything has its trade offs. Investing in growth has required being careful about how you invested your time and resources. You needed to cultivate a high level of efficiency as you sustained your level of success and added new growth opportunities. You couldn't afford to waste time if you were going to succeed in your job while going to school at night. How you invested every moment became important. You learned to take a book with you wherever you went, and to use every available minute to read your school work. You couldn't take that trip you have always wanted to take, or spend money without being careful as to what you spent it on. You learned how to deny yourself things that weren't helpful in advancing your life. Your discipline has become strong through practice. Notice the role discipline plays in growing your life.

TASK: List five things you are currently denying yourself because they aren't helpful in moving your life in the right direction.

EXERCISE 4B – DILIGENCE, GROWING

Exercise 4 invites you to see that those who are diligent demonstrate a well-seasoned discipline in all they do. Not only do they have a goal and a plan for almost every area of their life, they consistently follow those plans. There is seriousness to how they make decisions. They have taught themselves that it is critical to not deviate from the plan they established for their life, and won't let anything cause them to deviate from that plan. They rarely, if ever, succumb to the temptation to blow off the plan to splurge on something that doesn't advance them toward their goals. Those who are less diligent have more difficulty following through on their intentions. Because they are relatively content with where they are, they are less careful with their resources and are willing to indulge in expenditures of time and money that don't necessarily make life better in any meaningful way. They are more impulsive and indulgent.

TASK: Rate your level of diligence, with regard to being disciplined to stay on course, from 1 (highly disciplined) to 5 (not disciplined at all).

SESSION 3

EXERCISE 1C – DILIGENCE, GROWING

Session 3 focuses your attention on ways lack of greater diligence might be impeding your ability to thrive. While you are sufficiently diligent to continue to expand your life, you may need to expand your diligence to move to the next level. Let's get started.

Exercise 1 invites you to notice if you have some areas of laziness or resignation that are inhibiting your ambition to move into thriving. Thriving isn't easy. To live at that high level of performance, you must have sufficient ambition to keep taking on difficult and demanding challenges, and to surrender comforts and ease that you enjoy. While you have demonstrated the commitment to growing, you may not have enough ambition to move beyond it. You can determine your degree of resignation by identifying your dreams for the expansion of your life, and then making an honest assessment about your passion to go there.

TASK: List your dreams. How excited are you about them?

EXERCISE 2C – DILIGENCE, GROWING

Exercise 2 invites you to determine if you have any fears that are holding you back. You have been fearless in pushing yourself to grow. Even though you may have been anxious about all that would be expected of you, it did not stop you from pressing on. But, now you may be facing an issue that so frightens you, that it might overwhelm your desire to thrive. You may have some issue that you sense you will need to give up that you aren't willing to surrender. You may have to face the fact your marriage isn't the kind of partnership you need and, even though it isn't bad, you know you may run the risk of losing it if you keep pressing on.

TASK: Make a list of any issues that might feel like too much to face for you to move toward thriving.

EXERCISE 3C – DILIGENCE, GROWING

Exercise 3 invites you to notice if you have any areas of indulgence or temptations that are getting in the way of your thriving. You have been quite diligent in most areas of your life, but there may be one or two areas where you indulge yourself even though you know doing so is holding you back. You might say to yourself that you have given up enough to get where you are, and that it is okay to hold onto this one thing. And, you are right. You aren't obligated to press forward toward being your very best self, but if you are committed to living up to all of your potential, you will need to face those few indulgences that you are not dealing with. You will have to decide that having all of your life is worth more than whatever pleasure you get from giving into your temptation.

TASK: Spend some time getting clear with yourself. Don't turn away from what comes to your mind. Make a list of any indulgences or temptations that are holding you back.

EXERCISE 4C – DILIGENCE, GROWING

Exercise 4 invites you to notice if there are any gaps in your self-discipline that need to be repaired, or ways your self-discipline needs to be strengthened. It is difficult to be constantly vigilant and to hold yourself to such a high standard of discipline. There may be times or circumstances where you just want a break. Unless you deal with yourself with respect and grace, you can set yourself up for real problems. We are certain you have read stories about the pious evangelist who is caught in adultery, or the diligent accountant who has swindled money from his business. If you aren't careful, your discipline can "blow out" in ways that undermine all of the progress you have made. Notice where you are too harsh with yourself, or where you demand too much of yourself. These are areas where you are at risk for problems.

TASK: Make a list of any areas of your life where you feel your self-discipline is at risk for blowing up.

SESSION 4

EXERCISE 1D – DILIGENCE, GROWING

Session 4 focuses your attention on things you can do to become more diligent. Strengthening your diligence will allow you to overcome whatever obstacle is holding you back from thriving. Let's get started.

Exercise 1 invites you to become clearer about your potential. There are ways that you are extraordinary which, at times, become very clear to you. Whether it shows up in your insight in solving business problems, your compassion with your difficult neighbor, your ability to put a soccer ball in the goal, your understanding of how to lead others, or some other gift, when you are in that space you are amazing. The reason to push for thriving is because it is only when you have so carefully shaped your life that your giftedness will shine most brightly.

TASK: Consider your potential and what it might be like if it is shining fully. Write down whatever comes to you. Use this vision of your potential to motivate you to keep moving forward.

EXERCISE 2D – DILIGENCE, GROWING

Exercise 2 invites you to face your fears boldly. It is normal to be afraid. No one faces challenges without concern for failing. No one leaves behind the comfort of what is known to move into the unknown without trepidation. While experiencing fear is normal, how you deal with fear makes all the difference. If fear stops you in your tacks it will prevent you from thriving, but if you acknowledge your fear, breathe, and keep moving forward, fear won't hold you back from being your very best self.

TASK: Use your list of things you fear. Imagine facing each issue on your list with courage, pressing past it and arriving at a new, and better, place. Practice doing this every day until you have conquered your fear.

EXERCISE 3D – DILIGENCE, GROWING

Exercise 3 invites you to move past your temptations and self-indulgence. Certainly, it is natural to enjoy pleasure and to indulge in things you enjoy. You should do so as much as you can, but not when doing so gets in the way of where you need to go. There is a time for indulgence and there is a time for putting indulgence away. As you look at your list of temptations and indulgences, consider carefully what it is costing you to give in to these things. Do you feel good about your decisions? If you do, give up your goal of thriving and be content growing. If not, prepare yourself for greater diligence.

TASK: Imagine your life without the indulgence. Decide when you will give it up. Consider how much stronger your life will be without it. Now, act. Make different decisions about your temptations and indulgences.

EXERCISE 4D – DILIGENCE, GROWING

Exercise 4 invites you to cultivate even stronger self-discipline. It is easy to consider your self-discipline in comparison to that of others, and to feel so superior that you overlook the fact that it could and, perhaps should, be stronger still. Your self-discipline is meant to be your friend, helping you to stick with the path that leads to the very best for you. It only deprives you of what gets in the way of your best self. It supports you when you are tempted to stray and are weary. It needs to be exercised every day in big and small ways so it is ready to assist you when you need it the most.

TASK: Make a list of some ways you can exercise your self-discipline in ways you aren't doing now. Put them into play.

EXERCISE SERIES: MYOPIA

FACTOR – MYOPIA

This trait points to the degree to which we are teachable, see the big picture, and allow our point of view to be shaped by perspective and balance.

SELF-ASSESSED RATING - HANGING ON

You have a very narrow view of your life and of the world around you, and it is full of distortion.

SESSION 1

EXERCISE 1A – MYOPIA, HANGING ON

You are hanging on by your fingernails, at least partly, because you are extremely myopic. These exercises are designed to help you understand the concept of myopia, how it is undermining your life, and how you can begin to correct it. Session 1 focuses your attention only on the concept itself. Let's get started.

Exercise 1 invites you to understand that the key trait of myopia is the inability to see the big picture. Instead, people who suffer from myopia, most often only view their lives through a small point of view such as everything that is happening in their lives is impacting them. They can be extremely self-focused.

TASK: See if you can notice myopia in others. Listen for how people miss so much that is going on because they are only focused on a small picture.

EXERCISE 2A – MYOPIA, HANGING ON

Exercise 2 invites you to understand that because myopia limits the amount of information a person sees and processes, their point of view is often distorted and limited. If there are 100 things to see but you only see 10 of them, whatever conclusion you draw about what is going on is far more likely to be wrong than it is to be right. Hence, people who are myopic suffer from severe distortion. They are inclined to hold a point of view with which few agree, and so are often viewed as odd and out of step.

TASK: Pay attention to people's point of view, and see how many times you hear someone say something that is distorted because they don't see the bigger picture.

EXERCISE 3A – MYOPIA, HANGING ON

Exercise 3 invites you to understand that people who suffer from myopia are often quite unteachable. Not only is their point of view wildly distorted, they cling to their views tenaciously. They have no ability to see how different their thinking is from others, and often hold the view that they are right and everyone else is wrong. Rather than wondering if their idiosyncratic views need correcting, they prefer to believe that they are the only ones who see things correctly. Efforts to inform, correct, or teach such people are often met with resistance, defensiveness, and anger.

TASK: Pay attention to the people around you who are often wrong in their views. Notice how open they are to feedback and correction.

EXERCISE 4A – MYOPIA, HANGING ON

Exercise 4 invites you to understand how people who suffer from myopia are prone to see themselves as victims and to believe the world is against them. While they don't see the big picture, come to distorted conclusions about the world around them, hold fanciful points of view, and resist correction, they are likely to see that life isn't working well for them. Wherever they go people are different from them. The lives of other people obviously work better than do theirs. Their failure to connect with people, to relate effectively, and to align with reality undermines their lives at work as well as at home and with friends. It is no wonder they are hanging on by their fingernails.

TASK: See if you can identify people you know who suffer from myopia and are paying the price with the difficulty they experience in ordinary living. Notice how difficult it is for them to relate effectively to the world around them.

SESSION 2

EXERCISE 1B – MYOPIA, HANGING ON

Session 2 applies the concept of myopia to your life so you can better recognize when you are in its grip. Let's get started.

Exercise 1 invites you to see that when you have very strong opinions and strongly held views, you are likely to be suffering from myopia. There is so much to know that you don't know. If you were aware of how much you don't know, it would be difficult to be certain about anything. When you act as if you are certain, you are betraying your inability or unwillingness to see what you don't see.

TASK: Over the next three days, keep a log of the times you express very strong opinions and convictions.

EXERCISE 2B – MYOPIA, HANGING ON

Exercise 2 invites you to notice how often you get into strong disagreements with others. When you suffer from myopia and hold very strong opinions, you will often find yourself disagreeing with others. Those who are able to see more than you will see the world more clearly than do you, and so will rarely agree with your point of view. Because you don't see what they see, you will not be able to comprehend what they are telling you. Disagreements will ensue.

TASK: Over the next three days, keep a list of how often you get into disagreements and arguments with others. Do you appear more argumentative than most other people you know?

EXERCISE 3B – MYOPIA, HANGING ON

Exercise 3 invites you to notice that you frequently make mistakes in judgment. Because you don't see the bigger picture, your decisions and judgments are based on limited and incomplete information. Hence, they will often be wrong. What you expect to happen is likely not to occur. What you don't expect to happen might happen with some frequency. Whether or not you like to admit it, you are out of step with the world around you. You lack the ability to effectively align with what is occurring. It is very difficult to make effective decisions when you are myopic.

TASK: Make a list of 10 decisions you have made that didn't turn out as you expected. Write down what you expected to happen, and then what actually happened. How many of your mistakes had positive versus negative outcomes?

EXERCISE 4B – MYOPIA, HANGING ON

Exercise 4 invites you to see that you have a strong need to believe that you are right. Perhaps one of the worst symptoms of myopia is to be so strongly attached to your point of view even though it is wrong. You likely lack the ability to reflect on how frequently your judgments lead to unpredictable and negative outcomes, and to wonder if perhaps you are missing something. Instead, you tend to double down on your opinions and become stubbornly attached. This lack of receptivity to feedback and unwillingness to grasp your limitation makes it difficult for you to understand how you are getting in your own way.

TASK: Rate your need to be right from 1 (excessive) to 5 (hardly ever).

SESSION 3

EXERCISE 1C – MYOPIA, HANGING ON

Session 3 focuses your attention on some of the ways myopia is undermining your life. Let's get started.

Your inability to see the big picture results in a pattern of making poor life decisions. It isn't that you intend to make bad decisions. In fact, they seem like very good decisions to you. But, most of the time they don't work out as you expected. Instead, they frequently don't lead anywhere. You invest money in an investment you are convinced is secure and lose everything. You pay too much for your home and find yourself unable to move. You think what you are doing will win your boss' support only to discover it eroded his confidence in you. This pattern of poor decisions makes it impossible for you to create a strong and good life.

TASK: Track the pattern of your decisions over the past two years. Which have strengthened your life and which ones have eroded it?

EXERCISE 2C – MYOPIA, HANGING ON

Exercise 2 invites you to notice how difficult it is for you to build and maintain effective relationships. Your strong opinions and rigid way of seeing things might or might not attract attention, but it will make it almost impossible to maintain the interests of others. People will experience you as narrow-minded, judgmental, and ignorant. They will quickly tire of your rigidity and your insistence on being right. As people lose interest in you, they will move on and leave you behind. The result for you will be a shrinking circle of contacts and relationships.

TASK: Make a list of the relationships you have lost because of your myopia. Notice how valuable many of those people were when you were connected to them.

EXERCISE 3C – MYOPIA, HANGING ON

Exercise 3 invites you to notice that your life is progressively more lost as time goes by. You might have believed you had a bright future but your myopia is taking all of those possibilities from you. Your options are shrinking. Your social circle is dwindling. Your bad decisions have taken a toll on your finances. Your career has stalled and is in decline. Unless you expand your ability to see what is really going on, you will be unable to reverse the decline.

TASK: Make a list of five ways your life is in decline. Notice how long these patterns have been in place, and the potential consequences for your life if you don't change.

EXERCISE 4C – MYOPIA, HANGING ON

Exercise 4 invites you to notice your inability to understand how things got so bad or why your life is in such trouble. Your myopia limits your ability to see the truth. You can't easily see your role in undermining your own life. You would like to believe it is due to circumstances beyond your control, but hopefully, through these exercises you may begin to see that your inability to see the big picture is the cause of your problems.

TASK: Make a list of the people and circumstances you have blamed for the fact that your life is in disarray.

SESSION 4

EXERCISE 1D – MYOPIA, HANGING ON

Session 4 focuses your attention on some basic things you can do to become less myopic. Let's get started.

Exercise 1 invites you to open your eyes, so as to see yourself as responsible for all of the good and all that is not good in your life. This is the most important step you can take to begin to change. Until you can see that you are the one who has the power to make your life better, you will be waiting for someone or something to rescue you. Everyone who sees the world accurately understands the fundamental responsibility for shaping her life.

TASK: Complete this sentence 10 times: "I am responsible for __________." See if you can list both negative and positive things.

EXERCISE 2D – MYOPIA, HANGING ON

Exercise 2 invites you to open your eyes to all that you don't know. While it is impossible to see all that you don't know, the exercise of trying is quite expansive. If there is so much you don't know, how can you be certain of anything? Seeing the bigger picture softens your judgments and allows you to consider options. Slowing down and looking around before you speak and act will allow you to take in more information, and so to make more informed and accurate decisions.

TASK: Pick one issue you are facing. Make a list of at least 10 things that might be related to that issue that you don't know about. Consider how what you don't know might shape how you deal with the issue.

EXERCISE 3D – MYOPIA, HANGING ON

Exercise 3 invites you to value being curious. Curiosity moves you away from being myopic. There is so much to be curious about. You can be curious about the view and opinions of others. Become curious about different cultures, philosophies, and lifestyles. Become curious about things you don't know how to do, like fixing the brakes on your car, building a shed, or planting grass seed. Curiosity invites new information and new information expands your vision.

TASK: Make a list of 10 things about which you might be curious. Now do some investigating in those areas.

EXERCISE 4D – MYOPIA, HANGING ON

Exercise 4 invites you to ask questions. Asking questions is a powerful tool to move you out of myopia. Asking questions is the opposite of stating your opinions. In order to ask good questions, it is best to suspend your judgments. Use your questions to explore that which you are curious about. Ask people to tell you about their work. Listen and try to see things through their eyes. Ask more questions to better understand what they are telling you. Try on their point of view as if it were a new pair of shoes. See if you can fit yourself into their story. Questions will greatly expand your point of view of the world around you.

TASK: Practice asking 15 questions each day for the next week.

FACTOR – MYOPIA

This trait points to the degree to which we are teachable, see the big picture, and allow our point of view to be shaped by perspective and balance.

SELF-ASSESSED RATING - ERODING

Your view of yourself and of the world is too narrow for you to see the opportunities necessary to build a stable life.

SESSION 1

EXERCISE 1A – MYOPIA, ERODING

Your life is eroding, at least in part, because you suffer from myopia; the inability to see the big picture and to use that point of view to effectively shape your life. These exercises are designed to help you understand the concept of emotional myopia, see how it is showing up in your life, see the consequences of being myopic, and understand what you can do to begin to grow past it. Session 1 focuses your attention on the concept. Let's get started.

Exercise 1 invites you to understand that those who are myopic have a fairly narrow and predetermined view of life. It is almost as if they are able and willing to see only those things that confirm what they already believe. Hence their life is, in many ways, self-fulfilling. When they believe something will be difficult, all they can see is the difficulty. They will miss whatever is easy about the task.

TASK: This week notice the people around you and see how many you can find who demonstrate the limitation of seeing only what they predetermine to be the case.

EXERCISE 2A – MYOPIA, ERODING

Exercise 2 invites you to see that those who suffer from myopia demonstrate a fairly strong rigidity in how they view the world and live their lives. They have strong beliefs and opinions about many things and rarely change those attitudes.

They come across as if life has a "rule book" that they have mastered. They know how everything works and how things are done. They are likely to dominate conversations with their opinions, but not be very good at dialog that requires changing their mind or altering their opinion. They gravitate to organizations that have a clearly defined identity and may be leaders in such organizations.

TASK: This week, see how many people you know come across as very rigid in their thinking.

EXERCISE 3A – MYOPIA, ERODING

Exercise 3 invites you to see that those who are myopic demonstrate insensitivity to others. They aren't good at reading people and adapting in social situations. They can't easily tell when someone is becoming irritated, frustrated, or angry until it becomes quite obvious. Even then, they don't understand the reason people are upset. It is almost as if they are blind to the body language and tone of voice of their audience, because they are so focused on their own point of view and opinions. Even if they do see others reacting negatively to something they are saying or doing, those who are myopic lack the ability to adjust to create better outcomes. Hence, they don't do well in environments where there is much give and take, and where sharing points of view to reach a better outcome is required.

TASK: This week, notice how many people you know demonstrate this insensitivity to others or the ability to adjust in social situations.

EXERCISE 4A – MYOPIA, ERODING

Exercise 4 invites you to notice that those who are strongly myopic are often caught by surprise when things don't turn out well. They have difficulty seeing that subtle signs that indicate things aren't working out. Those who aren't myopic can see very early when things aren't going well at work. There are obvious signs, like projects that have a poor outcome, negative feedback, bad reviews, and demotion. And, there are subtle cues, like getting less attention from your supervisors and being excluded from meetings. If you aren't myopic, you read the writing on the wall and begin to make changes. Those who are myopic don't see the inevitable coming. They miss or misread all of the signs and so are quite caught off guard when the boss lets them go. Lacking the ability to anticipate outcomes, they can't prepare.

TASK: This week see if you can notice any people you know who are caught off guard by unexpected outcomes.

SESSION 2

EXERCISE 1B – MYOPIA, ERODING

Session 2 focuses your attention on recognizing myopia in yourself. This may not be easy since by definition, myopia limits your ability to see the bigger picture. But, we encourage you to do your best to try to see what we are pointing out to you. Avoid your immediate response to dismiss these insights as untrue. Instead, try them on to see if and how they might be true of you. Let's get started.

Exercise 1 invites you to notice that you do have strong opinions and views about many things and tend to be rigid about them.

TASK: Make a list of things that you believe are important in your life. This should not be difficult for you. You might include your religion, political position, or view on the economy. Now, write out what is important to you about this issue. Finally, see if you can write out how you might be wrong in your point of view. This is likely to be the most difficult part of this exercise, and may help you to see that you have some very clear views that you hold fairly rigidly.

EXERCISE 2B – MYOPIA, ERODING

Exercise 2 invites you to notice that you are strongly opinionated in your interactions with others. It isn't necessarily that you mean to be overbearing, but you may often come across that way to others.

TASK: Try paying close attention to how people react when you are talking about something that is important to you. Notice if they are gaining interest or losing interest in talking to you. Notice if they are enjoying the conversation or becoming slightly frustrated. If you see people starting to lose interest, it is likely because you aren't taking their opinions sufficiently into account in your conversation. It feels too much like a one-way street to them. It is very important that you are able to notice this.

EXERCISE 3B – MYOPIA, ERODING

Exercise 3 invites you to notice that things fairly frequently don't work out as you expected. You lack good radar that sees the world around you, and so informs you as to what is headed your way before it gets to you. Hence, you don't adjust well, and often have to react in the moment to things that catch you by surprise. A person you consider a good and close friend may suddenly end your friendship. You might be demoted at work when you thought you were getting a raise. Your neighbor, who you thought really liked you, might stop talking to you. All of this may seem quite odd to you, as if it has no reasonable explanation.

TASK: Make a list of as many of these "surprises" as you can.

EXERCISE 4B – MYOPIA, ERODING

Exercise 4 invites you to notice how you resist new information that might cause you to doubt your beliefs or to change your mind. You might not notice how much you prefer to watch the news that supports your political views, and to avoid or scoff at shows that advocate opposite views. You may not see how much you prefer to hang out with people who are like you, and how much you avoid those who are quite different from you. You may not see how frequently you have the same conversation with the same people, and how rarely you invite others to share divergent views and to disagree with you. Cutting yourself off from conflicting views and new information limits your ability to see new things and to broaden your perspective.

TASK: Make a list of all of the ways you limit your exposure to new information and different points of view.

SESSION 3

EXERCISE 1C – MYOPIA, ERODING

Session 3 focuses your attention on the negative impact your myopia is having on your life. The more clearly you see the impact, the more motivated you will be to change. Let's get started.

Exercise 1 invites you to see that your myopia limits your ability to grow. Since most of your opinions and judgments are already formed, you aren't challenging yourself to see the world in new and bigger ways. You have stalled the process of change in your life. You might notice people around you engaged in new hobbies, interests, and activities while your life rarely changes in any meaningful way.

TASK: Make a list of the changes you have made in the past year. Compare your list to some of your friends. Can you see that you have less growth than many other people?

EXERCISE 2C – MYOPIA, ERODING

Exercise 2 invites you to see that your myopia puts you out of step with the world around you. More often than not, your interactions with others and with circumstances just don't work all that well. Your limited view makes it difficult to anticipate what is required of you, and limits your ability to be flexible. Hence, you either don't anticipate things well, or you can't make the needed adjustments. You might make mistakes like wearing the wrong clothes to the party, having the wrong assignment completed at work, or not having properly assessed how important your attendance was at a meeting. This inability to stay in step with the world is resulting in a life that is eroding.

TASK: List at least five examples of times you were out of step with the expectations of others.

EXERCISE 3C – MYOPIA, ERODING

Exercise 3 invites you to see that your myopia predictably leads to the decline in the quality and effectiveness of your life. Life is constantly changing around you and so requiring that you keep up. Unless you can see what is changing, how you need to change, and actually make those adjustments, you simply can't effectively move forward. The best you can hope for is to hold your current place, but unless you are moving forward, the current of life tends to drag you backward. Signs that your life is eroding are obvious in things like a progressively small social circle, a vocational life that is becoming less productive and useful, and a sense of being less relevant and useful than you used to be. These are serious issues. Until you stem the tide and begin moving forward, your life will be sliding into disrepair to the point where nothing can be done to turn it around.

TASK: List five symptoms that your life is in decline due to your inability to relate to the world around you in an effective manner.

EXERCISE 4C – MYOPIA, ERODING

Session 4 invites you to see that your myopia limits your ability to fit in, even when you see your life is in decline. Your habit of limiting your access to new information, and your desire to persist in ways of thinking that aren't working is making it difficult, if not impossible, to understand what you need to do to get your life on a better course. You may see the problems you are encountering, but don't see clearly what you can do to turn things around. Just as color blindness limits the ability to make good choices about clothing to wear, myopia limits the ability to make effective life choices. Hopefully, you see that you lack sufficient information to address the decline in your life. The next step is to open yourself to seeing the bigger picture so you can get on a more positive track.

TASK: Make a list of the things you imagine you need to know, but don't know, in order to make your life work better.

SESSION 4

EXERCISE 1D – MYOPIA, ERODING

Session 4 focuses your attention on ways you can address your myopia in order to stop your life from eroding and move toward a more stable and secure mode of living. Let's get started.

Exercise 1 invites you to always be seeking to notice when you are being myopic. Since you know you have the tendency to see the small picture and miss the big one, you would benefit from looking for ways that bias might be showing up. Always imagine that you might not be seeing everything there is to see. Ask yourself frequently what you might be missing. Question your opinions and judgments because you know they are built on a small subset of all of the relevant data.

TASK: Every day for the next week, practice watching for ways you are being myopic.

EXERCISE 2D – MYOPIA, ERODING

Exercise 2 invites you to welcome input from others. Because you know your perspective is limited, you would benefit from welcoming new information that may help you gain a more complete picture of all that is happening in your world. The people you know are a rich source of that new information. Practice asking people for their point of view. Listen to what they tell you with a generous curiosity. Notice when you begin to shut down and become defensive, and practice shifting to an more open posture. Practice laying out your thoughts to your friends and inviting them to tell you what you might be missing. As they become more used to your welcoming invitation, you will find they give their input even when you forget to ask.

TASK: Every day this week invite at least three people to give you input.

EXERCISE 3D – MYOPIA, ERODING

Exercise 3 invites you to always seek a bigger perspective. Because you know there is always more to know than you know, and more to see than you are seeing, become curious as to what you don't know. Value learning what you don't know above the certainty of what you know. Rather than quickly sharing your views, practice being quiet and listening. Take in whatever you hear and use that information to develop more complete points of view, as if you are discovering pieces of a jigsaw puzzle and each new piece allows you to see a more complete picture. Every day this week practice being quiet and listening.

TASK: Keep a list of everything you learn.

EXERCISE 4D – MYOPIA, ERODING

Exercise 4 invites you to value alignment with the world around you. Your life is eroding largely because you make decisions based on limited information. When you make alignment important, you seek to understand all you can about an issue before you act. For example, if you are buying a car, you might ask the salesperson the price and think you know it is a good deal. But, if you seek alignment, you might ask your friends for their thoughts about the price, check prices at various dealerships, and then check prices online. Your research may confirm that you were correct that the salesperson's price was a good one and you should close the deal. Or, it may reveal that the price was thousands of dollars too much, and you would have been cheated. It is only by questioning your thoughts and gathering information that you will be best aligned with the world.

TASK: Pick one decision that is currently important to you. What decision are you considering? Make a list of some research you can do before you decide. After you conduct your research, notice if you have changed your decision.

FACTOR – MYOPIA

This trait points to the degree to which we are teachable, able to see the big picture, and allow our point of view to be shaped by perspective and balance.

SELF-ASSESSED RATING - TREADING WATER

You have a big enough view of yourself and of the world to make decisions that support some success and stability.

SESSION 1

EXERCISE 1A – MYOPIA, TREADING WATER

You are treading water, at least partly, because you can be myopic. These exercises are designed to assist you in better understanding what it means to be myopic, identifying ways you are showing this trait, understanding how myopia might be holding you back from growing, and suggesting some ways you might become less myopic. Session 1 focuses your attention on my myopia means. Let's get started.

Exercise 1 invites you to see that people who are myopic assume they see the whole picture when they do not. Everyone is myopic to some extent because no one has access to all of the relevant information for any issue or problem they face. But the assumption of knowing more than you know sets you up for making errors.

TASK: Every day this week listen to your friends, neighbors, and coworkers talk. See if you can identify those who are prone to think they know more than they actually do.

EXERCISE 2A – MYOPIA, TREADING WATER

Exercise 2 invites you to notice that those who are myopic jump to conclusions too quickly. Possessing limited information makes decision-making easy, because there is such little data to take into account. Choosing between two options is much easier than choosing between 25. Often, people who suffer from some myopia are seen as decisive, though they aren't well conceived and balanced. It isn't that their thinking is unclear. Rather it is simplistic. Hence, time too often proves that their lack of sufficient information led to critical errors and mistakes.

TASK: Make a list of people you know who seem quite certain, but have made quick and clear decisions that turned out poorly because they didn't take enough information into account.

EXERCISE 3A – MYOPIA, TREADING WATER

Exercise 3 invites you to notice that those who are myopic miss essential connections. This is a typical "being stuck in the weeds" problem. You have your head down and only see that which is front of you. You are pretty good at dealing with the current situation, but because you aren't looking around, you don't see how what you are doing now is going to impact things in the future. You just don't see the connection. For example, you have the money to buy an expensive car, so you buy one. But, you didn't think about how you are going to need a new roof next year. When the roof starts leaking, you don't have the money to get it fixed. People who have myopia frequently suffer from these types of errors because they miss essential connections. They are too narrowly focused.

TASK: Pay attention to the people in your life. See if you can spot this pattern of seeing the weeds but missing the forest. See if you can identify some mistakes caused by this problem.

EXERCISE 4A – MYOPIA, TREADING WATER

Exercise 4 invites you to notice that those who are myopic often come to the wrong conclusions when they make decisions. It is so difficult to make good decisions when you have only a limited number of facts related to it. The more information you possess, the more perspectives you consider things from, and the more likely you will make the decision that serves you best. For example, someone tells you about a wonderful vacation they had in Italy. As you listen to them, you decide you would like to plan a similar trip, so you do. What you didn't ask about, and so didn't know, is that your friend is Italian and has family in Italy with whom she stayed. When you arrive, you are shocked at how expensive it is to stay there, and how difficult it is to get around because no one speaks your language. There were so many questions you should have asked. There was so much you needed to consider before planning your trip.

TASK: Notice those around you who tend to be myopic, and see if you can spot some poor decisions they have made because they lacked enough information.

SESSION 2

EXERCISE 1B – MYOPIA, TREADING WATER

Session 2 focuses your attention on how myopia might be showing up in your life and interfering with your ability to grow. You could not have built such a stable and secure life if you suffered greatly from this problem, but as you work your way through these exercises, you may begin to make connections between certain ways you think and behave, and ways you are limiting your life. Let's get started.

Exercise 1 invites you to see that you have a tendency to limit the focus of your attention to the life you have built for yourself. You know how to do what is required to maintain your job. You have routines at home that keep things in adequate repair and order. You have a group of friends with whom you are comfortable and whom you enjoy. You have built a good life, and you seem quite content with maintaining what you have. There is certainly nothing wrong with this point of view, but it doesn't set you up for growth.

TASK: Make a list of things you focus on that help you maintain your life as it is.

EXERCISE 2B – MYOPIA, TREADING WATER

Exercise 2 invites you to see that you don't tend to expand your thinking into the future or give much thought to expansion. Growth almost always requires expansion of thinking. Columbus didn't just board a ship and start sailing west. He spent many years thinking about the world, its shape, and a different way of getting to the Far East. You can imagine that all of this thinking about what he didn't have, was preparation for the expansion he created. He was preparing himself to move beyond the comfortable, and into the new. If you don't think much about a life beyond the one you currently enjoy, it isn't likely that you will create one.

TASK: Notice what you think about every day for the next week. How often do you find yourself contemplating a different job, home, neighborhood, social group, or hobby? Can you connect your lack of thinking beyond your current situation with the fact that you aren't growing?

EXERCISE 3B – MYOPIA, TREADING WATER

Exercise 3 invites you to see that you don't tend to create many growth experiences for yourself. You might say you easily fall into ruts. You may eat at the same restaurants, order the same dishes, shop in the same stores, and follow the same routine every day. Routines have their merit. They reduce the need to make decisions, but they also limit expansion and growth. The more new things you do, the more your world expands. This is true even in small ways. Simply driving to work on a different route exposes you to things you don't normally see. Eating at new restaurants and ordering different dishes broadens your experience.

TASK: Do an assessment of the choices you make over the next week. How many are routines that maintain the life you have now, compared to choices that create encounters with new and unfamiliar places, people, and events?

EXERCISE 4B – MYOPIA, TREADING WATER

Exercise 4 invites you to notice that you might actually become a bit defensive toward anything that pushes you out of your comfort zone. You like the life you have built. You may see no reason to move beyond it. And of course, the only reason to do so is to move toward releasing more of your potential, your greatness, into the world and into your life. But, rather than welcoming things that would expand your world, you may find that you become defensive. You argue with those who encourage you to try new things that it is unnecessary. You resist feedback, even the feedback you are getting in these exercises, telling yourself that it is wrong or that you aren't understood. Resistance is often a sign that you know there is some truth in what you are hearing that you aren't quite ready to face.

TASK: See if you can list five signs of being defensive to forces that are encouraging you to grow.

SESSION 3

EXERCISE 1C – MYOPIA, TREADING WATER

Session 3 focuses your attention on some of the implications of your myopia on your life. You may assume that resisting growth will not impact the pleasant life you have built. That may be naïve. Let's get started.

Exercise 1 invites you to see that you squander opportunities. Life does not offer you an endless supply of opportunities to grow. Every time you pass on an opportunity to grow, you have one less. You can clearly see this to be the case if you look back at your life. You thought about being a cheerleader, but didn't go out for the team. Certainly, that isn't the end of the world, but you have no idea how joining the team might have changed your life. It might have led to a life-long friendship that was never built. It could have left you with a love for physical fitness or cheering that shaped your hobbies or career. These are all unknowns, but wasting opportunities may be more important than you realized.

TASK: Make a list of 10 opportunities for growth or change that you wasted.

EXERCISE 2C – MYOPIA, TREADING WATER

Exercise 2 invites you to notice that your myopia leads to a rather stagnant life. It isn't that your life is bad, but only that it isn't growing. Perhaps you remember how your grandparents' house smelled. It wasn't a bad smell, but the smell of two people who have lived the same way in the same place for a long time. It wasn't the smell of change and newness. It was the smell of stagnation. Perhaps your life has a similar smell, but it is one with which you have become so accustomed that you don't notice it.

TASK: You can best determine the stagnation of your life by making a list of the 10 biggest changes you have made in your life over the past five years. If they are big changes, like going back to school, writing a book, or backpacking through France, your life probably doesn't have much of a smell. On the other hand, if your big changes were changing out the carpet in the living room and changing banks, you might imagine your life could be stagnating.

EXERCISE 3C – MYOPIA, TREADING WATER

Exercise 3 invites you to notice that your myopia atrophies your ability to expand and to grow. Growth requires the courage to change, and the ability to continually let go of what is comfortable for the possibility of something better or different. There is a part of each of us that would like to stop, be content, and to settle. As your myopia limits your ability to see beyond what you have now, you aren't exercising your courage and conviction to grow. Without exercise, those parts of yourself will shrink and become weak. You will become increasingly resistant to change and more complacent in accepting things as they are. Look back to your life years ago.

TASK: List changes you made when you were a child. Can you see that you were more courageous then in growing your life than you are now?

EXERCISE 4C – MYOPIA, TREADING WATER

Exercise 4 invites you to notice that your myopia is causing you to be left behind. When you compare your life to that of some of your more successful friends, you might come to see that they are always looking for the next thing they need to take on and then moving in that direction, while your life has changed very little by comparison.

TASK: Pick someone you know who has a life that seems richer than your own. Make a list of the changes you have noticed the making. Consider a variety of areas of life, including their occupation and job function, health and fitness, lifestyle, and experiences. Then, compare that list to your own. Can you see that you are allowing yourself to be left behind? Those who are growing are moving beyond you.

SESSION 4

EXERCISE 1D – MYOPIA, TREADING WATER

Sessions 4 focuses your attention on ways you can begin to grow past your myopia. Some will be exercises to change how you see the world and think about life. Others will be recommended actions you can take to open your eyes. Let's get started.

Exercise 1 invites you to feed your desire for growth. You may frequently look only at what you have accomplished and at what you possess and congratulate yourself. "We have three wonderful children who are doing well. Our life is great!" You might not as often ask yourself what is next for your life and where you want to go. "We have done a great job of raising three children. What shall we take on next?" If you feed your desire for growth, opportunities will appear.

TASK: Start talking to your family and friends about growing, changing, and learning. Introduce this theme into conversations at least three times each day for the next month.

EXERCISE 2D – MYOPIA, TREADING WATER

Exercise 2 invites you to consider how you see the world. When you are myopic, you tend to see the world around you as dangerous and harsh. If the world is dangerous, why would you ever want to leave the security of the life you have built to venture into it? But, what if you saw the world as a playground, filled with opportunities for you to have fun and play? Would you not be more inclined to leave your safety? How you see the world is how the world will show up for you. If you are looking for danger, you will see it everywhere. But, if you are looking for adventure, growth, and change, you will see opportunities for those experiences everywhere.

TASK: Practice saying to yourself, "The world is my playground" at least five times a day, each day for a month.

EXERCISE 3D – MYOPIA, TREADING WATER

Exercise 3 invites you to seek change as frequently as you can. Practice breaking old habits by doing things that are different and new. Rearrange your bedroom furniture. That isn't a big thing, but notice how differently you feel when you walk into your bedroom. Drive to and from work by a different route. It doesn't matter if it is longer. Notice the things you see that you didn't along the old route. Sit in a different chair when you eat dinner. The more frequently you make these small changes, the more you will strengthen your ability to take on bigger changes.

TASK: Make a list of five small changes you are willing to make.

EXERCISE 4D – MYOPIA, TREADING WATER

Exercise 4 invites you to embrace risk. Risk is simply change that feels a bit uncertain. Rearranging your bedroom furniture is a change, but not a risk. Visiting a foreign country might be a risk, especially if you don't travel extensively. Risk is a necessary part of growth because growth is unknown. Your life will change in unexpected ways. The more you practice taking risks, the more comfortable you will get with doing so and the more you will be willing to embrace bigger ones. Risks move you out of your comfort zone toward something new that you want. You might join a class to learn a foreign language. You might fail the class and feel badly about yourself. You can protect yourself from that risk by not taking the class, or you can embrace the risk and see how things go. If you succeed in learning that new language, visiting a country that speaks that language may seem like a more acceptable risk to take next.

TASK: Make a list of five risks you are willing to take.

FACTOR – MYOPIA

This trait points to the degree to which we are teachable, see the big picture, and allow our point of view to be shaped by perspective and balance.

SELF-ASSESSED RATING - GROWING

You have a large enough view of yourself and the world to see opportunities that expand your life.

SESSION 1

EXERCISE 1A – MYOPIA, GROWING

You are growing in your life because you are usually able to see the bigger picture and relate to it effectively. However, you may have some symptoms of myopia that keep you from thriving. These exercises are designed to assist you in pinpointing precisely where you may be being myopic, understanding how it is holding you back, and then overcoming your myopia so you can shift into thriving. People who are growing see many things clearly, but they sometimes suffer from "selective myopia." They have blind spots where they have distortion or an unwillingness to understand. Session 1 focuses on helping you gain a better understanding of some of these blind spots. Let's get started.

Exercise 1 invites you to see that emotion can sometimes overwhelm the ability to see clearly. Perhaps you know someone who seems quite rational and reasonable until something touches a nerve. Suddenly, it is as if their mind shuts down. They stop listening. They aren't open to anyone or anything. It is as they are possessed by their emotions.

TASK: This week, see if you notice anyone demonstrating myopia driven by uncontrolled emotion. This can occur over all kinds of issues like politics, religion, or even certain people.

EXERCISE 2A – MYOPIA, GROWING

Exercise 2 invites you to notice that "selective myopia" can occur in connection with people in your life. You might be quite rational and balanced with almost everyone, but with your ex, or your old boss, you go nuts. You have all kinds of judgments. You have no balance in your point of view. You are at the effect of your emotions. You aren't willing to entertain the idea that you might be biased. Such a narrow point of view about a person or persons in your life limits your ability to see a bigger picture, and can cause you to make mistakes in judgments or to miss opportunities. It doesn't take many of these emotionally charged relationships to divert you from thriving.

TASK: Make a list of all of the people in your life that trigger myopia for you. You don't have to see these people to have this reaction. Only thinking about them is enough.

EXERCISE 3A – MYOPIA, GROWING

Exercise 3 invites you to notice that "selective myopia" can occur as a result of insecurities. You might typically exude strong confidence in yourself and your ability to build a strong and successful life except when it comes to ___________. For whatever reason, you may have some area of insecurity that, when experienced, so becomes the focus of your attention that you lose the ability to see the big picture. You could have stage fright. When you are asked to present on subject matter of which you are an expert, you begin to sweat and get tongue-tied. The worry about looking silly or doing a poor job overwhelms your ability to see that you are quite skilled with the material you are presenting.

TASK: Make a list of insecurities that might be holding you back from thriving because they take over your thinking and limit your ability to be objective.

EXERCISE 4A – MYOPIA, GROWING

Exercise 4 invites you to notice that "selective myopia" can occur as a result of fear. Some people have a fear of snakes, spiders, heights, or closed spaces. Even the thought of such things triggers a constricting of thought and a wave of panic. Fear has a way of expanding and taking over more and more of your thinking.

Certainly, you have had that experience. You might be out on a date with your spouse and the thought comes into your head that something is wrong at home. There is no reason to be afraid, but you can't get the idea out of your head. Now, the date isn't fun at all. You don't taste what you are eating and can't think of anything to talk about except going home. The fear triggered "selective myopia" limited your ability to enjoy your date.

TASK: List all of the fears you have that might hold you back from thriving.

SESSION 2

EXERCISE 1B – MYOPIA, GROWING

Your myopia is not keeping you from growing. You are embracing change and new opportunities. But, there may be certain things that you avoid or that you miss because of your "selective myopia." Session 2 focuses your attention on four of those issues. Let's get started.

Exercise 1 invites you to see to the extent you become triggered and overwhelmed with emotion, you are always vulnerable to becoming unsettled and out of balance. Regardless of whether the trigger is politics, your favorite sports team, or your ex, your vulnerability to that issue puts you at risk of missing whatever opportunity is available in that moment. You will not see it because you are completely preoccupied with your emotional disturbance. You could be having a conversation that might have led to a new business deal, but when you went off about the election, the conversation never returned to business. You have no idea how many opportunities you might have missed because of you were upset.

TASK: List five opportunities you know you missed because you became too emotional.

EXERCISE 2B – MYOPIA, GROWING

Exercise 2 invites you to see that to the extent you are triggered by certain people in your life, you limit your social interaction. Having negative energy toward people, regardless of whom they are and what they have done, hurts you more than it hurts them. Perhaps you have a grievance toward someone at work. You don't like them and believe they are out to get you. You used to be friendly, but now you are on guard around them. When you see them coming down the hall, you duck into a room so you don't have to greet them. You complain about them to others. You have no idea how much time you are wasting and how this anger and resentment is shaping how you relate to other people at work. You have allowed this unresolved relationship to bias how you build your social connections.

TASK: List five ways some resentment toward someone in your life is affecting how you relate to the world.

EXERCISE 3B – MYOPIA, GROWING

Exercise 3 invites you to see how your insecurities may be holding you back from thriving. Perhaps you are insecure about your athletic ability. You know this is not one of your strengths, but you aren't accepting of your level of athletic prowess. Instead, you worry that you will stand out and won't be accepted. At your company picnic, everyone is talking about a friendly softball game. Suddenly, you become very uncomfortable. The idea of playing softball with your peers sounds like a very bad idea. You will look weird if you refuse to play, and you fear you will look weird if you do. Now, the picnic isn't fun at all. The idea of the game was meant to be fun, but it isn't fun for you at all. This is how insecurity limits your ability to thrive in whatever situation you find yourself.

TASK: List five times you recall limiting your ability to be fully in the moment because you felt insecure.

EXERCISE 4B – MYOPIA, GROWING

Exercise 4 invites you to see the consequences of your fear on your limitation to fully thrive. It doesn't matter what you fear; fear will always limit your ability to live freely and fully. It is the nature of fear. Fear is designed to protect you from things you anticipate happening. It manages those contingencies by preparing you to deal with whatever might occur, even though many of those things aren't likely to happen. That whole process limits your ability to be fully present to what is happening. Imagine you are preparing a presentation to the PTA. You fear it not going well. Your mind begins to generate possible ways it could go poorly so you can prepare to deal with them. Now, you are preparing for multiple possible reactions, and are feeling scattered and unable to fully focus. Your natural ability to show up, be relaxed, and connect is muted.

TASK: List five ways your fear has limited your life.

SESSION 3

EXERCISE 1C – MYOPIA, GROWING

Session 3 focuses your attention on some shifts you can make that will begin to free you from whatever myopia has been holding you back from thriving. Let's get started.

Exercise 1 invites you to up the ante. Growing is good, but not good enough. You can grow while still maintaining some of your old baggage you identified in previous exercises. In order to move toward thriving, it is time to leave the old baggage behind. Myopia can't be maintained without paying a price. Anything and everything that limits the full release of your potential needs to be jettisoned. But, this is a decision. You may be comfortable with your level of success. Or, your baggage may be so precious to you that you are willing to sacrifice thriving to keep it. We respect your right to decide. But, we want you to make this a conscious decision. So, take a few days and consider carefully what you want to do.

TASK: Right now, set a date and time when you will decide.

EXERCISE 2C – MYOPIA, GROWING

Exercise 2 invites you to consider the importance of "clean energy." You experience "clean energy" when you have no internal conflicts or constraint. Your life energy is only positive and free flowing. You may experience clean energy with a child, especially when they are young, or with your dog who adores you. You have no hidden resentment, mixed motive, or secrets. However, in other relationships, you may lack "clean energy." You may be holding back feelings that are negative and angry. You may be harboring jealousy or envy. You may be keeping secrets or holding grudges. Only you can release yourself from negative energy. The very first step in doing so is to acknowledge it to yourself.

TASK: Make a list of all of the issues and people where you have less than "clean energy."

EXERCISE 3C – MYOPIA, GROWING

Exercise 3 invites you to master the power of forgiveness. Forgiveness is one way to create clean energy in relationships. Forgiveness is appropriate when someone has truly harmed you in some way. Harm happens with people. We do things to each other, both intentionally and unintentionally, that does harm. It is almost impossible to be in a close relationship for any period of time without creating some harm, whether serious or not. Harboring resentment toward someone who has harmed you can feel powerful. You are in the position to punish the offender by holding a grudge and maintaining righteous indignation. But, holding your resentment keeps you both stuck in negative energy. Forgiveness is as simple as letting go of whatever you are holding. By releasing your resentment, you free yourself to move on. You know you have let it go when you have no emotional energy about the issue or person.

TASK: Practice exercising forgiveness this week by forgiving at least three people for something you have been holding against them.

EXERCISE 4C – MYOPIA, GROWING

Exercise 4 invites you to master reconciliation. Sometimes forgiveness is not enough to free you from the myopia that is limiting the freedom to live your life as freely and fully as is possible. Not only do you need to let go of whatever resentment you have been holding, but you also need to build a more useful and free relationship. You may be in the grip of some story you have been holding. For example, you have forgiven your husband for the ugly things he said about you when he was angry, but you have a story about him that he harbors resentment toward you. As long as you maintain that story, you read almost everything he does though that lens and see hidden resentment. Reconciliation calls you to share the story you have about him with him, and admit it isn't necessarily true; it is only your story. Next, tell him what you want; "an open, trusting relationship." Do this until you feel free of the grip of your story.

TASK: Identify two people with whom you want to reconcile, and practice sharing your story and what you want.

SESSION 4

EXERCISE 1D – MYOPIA, GROWING

Session 4 focuses you on four final skills that will help you release any remaining myopia so you can move toward a life of fully thriving. Let's get started.

Exercise 1 invites you to shift your focus from inward to outward. Insight and self-understanding are important. But, understanding the world and relating effectively to it is just as important, if not more so. The effort to get others to understand you better and to accept you more, is not nearly as useful as coming to understand the world better and learning to accept it. Life is not there for you. You have the privilege of experiencing life. You can spend your existence battling the current by constantly swimming upstream, all the while complaining that the current is flowing the wrong direction, or you can notice where the current flows, join it, and be carried along almost effortlessly. The choice is yours. Those who are not myopic are excellent at reading the current and fitting into it. Their lives flow easefully. They are always changing themselves to make their lives more effective.

TASK: Make a list of issues over which you are too focused on yourself, and not sufficiently focused on the world outside yourself. This week, practice shifting your focus on two of those issues.

EXERCISE 2D – MYOPIA, GROWING

Exercise 2 invites you to cultivate courage. Courage is simply the power or quality of dealing with or facing danger, fear, and pain. When you are committed to thriving, you accept that the journey of life will include danger, fear and pain. Suffering is part of the experience of life. If you choose to try to avoid suffering, you must limit how you live. You will be imposing myopia on yourself. But, if you accept suffering and face it with courage, you open the way for thriving. One clear example of courage is the decision for a woman to have a child. The path of carrying and giving birth is filled with danger, fear, and pain. It takes courage to step into such an experience. But, for the joy of being a mother and of raising a child, she embraces the path with courage.

TASK: Make a list of areas you have been avoiding because you were afraid. Practice embracing them in a similar way a mother embraces giving birth.

EXERCISE 3D – MYOPIA, GROWING

Exercise 3 invites you to grow in grace. Grace is defined as unmerited favor. It means being kind and accepting even when it is undeserved. Grace gives you the power to open yourself to new experiences by releasing whatever is holding you back. For example, grace allows you to accept yourself just as you are. When you are good at extending grace toward yourself, your insecurities and sense of inadequacy completely disappear. They no longer have the ability to hold you back. When you master extending grace toward others, all resentment, jealousy, envy, and bitterness melts away. You no longer harbor any of the negative feelings that distract you from moving forward in your life. You cultivate grace through understanding and accepting weakness and fault. Each of us has the same capacity for good or for evil, to hurt and to heal. We are all in the same game of living life together. Rather than competing and comparing, we can offer acceptance, understanding, forgiveness, and grace.

TASK: Practice extending grace to yourself and to others. Keep a record of each time you do.

EXERCISE 4D – MYOPIA, GROWING

Exercise 4 invites you to grow in love. Love is the most powerful force on earth. It has the power to transform your life and the lives of everyone you encounter. Love is defined as an intense feeling of deep affection. When you love someone, you see them for their very best self. You do your best to act in their best interest. You do whatever you can to protect them from harm. You believe in them, support them, encourage them, and forgive them. Every one of us would benefit from loving ourselves more fully. We would also benefit greatly from loving everyone we meet more fully. This is not a very difficult task because there is so much room for improvement. It is truly a case of willingness.

TASK: If you want to grow past your myopia and into a place where you are fully thriving, practice loving everyone you meet today.

EXERCISE SERIES: EXPERIENCE SHARING

FACTOR – EXPERIENCE SHARING

The creation and telling of stories is part of the fabric of the human condition. Stories are no more than the meaning we make of the events in our lives. Our stories are, to some extent, always shaped by our past experiences and biases. We move toward Purpose when our stories inspire us to bring our best self into our work and lives, and when they support our understanding that our lives matter and that we can make a difference in the world. Our stories undermine our Purpose when they lead to bigotry, prejudice, selfishness, greed, envy, hatred, and all other attitudes that shrink our perspective and trap us in negativity and smallness.

SELF-ASSESSED RATING - HANGING ON

The stories you construct are filled with drama that diverts results in wasted energy and effort.

SESSION 1

EXERCISE 1A – EXPERIENCE SHARING, HANGING ON

Your life is not doing well largely because of how you deal with stories. We all make up stories about everything that happens in our lives. Stories are simply our interpretation of facts and include our biases, prejudices, and past experiences. Our stories can either support or undermine our ability to effectively relate to life. Rarely do we consider our stories and the impact they have on us. These exercises are designed to help you better understand that impact. Session 1 invites you to focus on the stories you might have about the world around you that may negatively impact your life. Let's get started.

Exercise 1 invites you to notice if you tell yourself stories that the world is unfair. These can show up around many issues, but almost always include the theme, "No matter what I do, I can't win because it isn't fair." Your stories might tell you that things aren't fair at work, so there is no reason to try to get ahead. You might think school isn't fair, so you could never graduate. Thinking that things are unfair undermines motivation to try to change things for the better.

TASK: Make a list of at least five times you catch yourself thinking or saying something isn't fair.

EXERCISE 2A – EXPERIENCE SHARING, HANGING ON

Exercise 2 invites you to consider how often your stories include the theme, "This is too hard for me." From time to time you might entertain the idea of doing something new and different like learning a new language, going back to school or losing 20 pounds, but almost immediately, the story arises in your mind, "I can't succeed at that. It is too hard for me." Rather than believing in your ability to learn and to master life, this story undermines your confidence in yourself. It makes it seem pointless to even try, because you are destined to fail. The "This is too hard for me" story can undermine your ability to take on almost any challenge. In this way, it limits your ability to grow and adapt to the demands of effective living.

TASK: Make a list of at least five times when you catch yourself thinking or saying, "It is too hard for me."

EXERCISE 3A – EXPERIENCE SHARING, HANGING ON

Exercise 3 invites you to notice how often your stories include the theme, "There is nothing I can do." This story is one of helplessness, as if circumstances are so set in stone that any action you take would have no effect on the outcome. And, since you can make no difference, there is no reason to try. The "There is nothing I can do" story feeds depression and despair. The longer you live with this story and the more frequently it shows up in your life, the less likely it is that you will do anything to try to better your circumstances. Instead, you will surrender to whatever is occurring and allow yourself to be overwhelmed by it. Instead of learning new skills at work, you will accept that layoffs are coming and allow yourself to be laid off. Because you don't believe there is anything you can do, you won't get another job. Life will get worse and worse.

TASK: Make a list of five times when you catch yourself saying or thinking, "There is nothing I can do."

EXERCISE 4A – EXPERIENCE SHARING, HANGING ON

Exercise 4 invites you to notice how often your stories include the theme, "It's not my fault." This is a common story that you might frequently tell yourself. Things happen to you and instead of seeing your part in creating them you say to yourself, "It isn't my fault." Those few words absolve you of any and all responsibility for whatever is occurring. And, because your story relieves you of all responsibility, you fail to see this as a learning opportunity to discover how you could be more effective in the future. Your story puts you in a frame of mind to excuse yourself rather than to better yourself.

TASK: Make a list of at least five times when you catch yourself thinking or saying, "It's not my fault."

SESSION 2

EXERCISE 1B – EXPERIENCE SHARING, HANGING ON

Session 2 focuses your attention on stories you may have about yourself that are causing your life to be in disarray. Let's get started.

Exercise 1 invites you to notice how often your stories include the theme, "I have made too many mistakes." There are variations on this theme but the basic idea is that you get only so many chances in life, and you have messed up so many that it is too late to do anything about it. Mistakes don't have to be seen as fatal unless your story requires it. Mistakes can also be seen as learning opportunities. But, when you are in the grip of this story, each mistake you make is like a cat losing one if its nine lives. Your story uses your mistakes as an excuse for not getting back in the game and doing things better.

TASK: Make a list of at least five times you catch yourself thinking or saying, "I have made too many mistakes."

EXERCISE 2B – EXPERIENCE SHARING, HANGING ON

Exercise 2 invites you to consider how often your stories include the theme, "I am not good enough." This is a very common and seriously detrimental story to create, because it sets artificial and arbitrary limits on how successful you can be and what you can achieve. You might hear the voice in your head saying, "I am not good enough for that job" or "I am not good enough for that person to want to date me." As soon as that story takes hold in your mind, the game is over. You will lack the confidence to apply for the job or to ask that person out on a date. The story that "You are not good enough," guts your self-confidence and so cripples your ability to make good things happen in your life.

TASK: Make a list of at least five times you catch yourself thinking or saying, "I am not good enough."

EXERCISE 3B – EXPERIENCE SHARING, HANGING ON

Exercise 3 invites you to notice how often your stories include the theme, "It is just too hard for me." There are variations on this theme. You might say "That is too much to expect of me," or "That's impossible," or "Your expectations are too high." Each of these stories contains the same basic message that you don't have what it takes to do what is being asked of you. That story sells you short. Rather than believing in yourself, which would draw out more potential, this story makes it very easy to pass on the opportunity because you expect failure.

TASK: Make a list of at least five times you catch yourself thinking or saying, "It is just too hard for me."

EXERCISE 4B – EXPERIENCE SHARING, HANGING ON

Exercise 4 invites you to notice how often your stories include the theme, "I have nothing to offer." Perhaps this is the most devastating story you can have about yourself, because it overlooks every positive attribute you possess and sums up all of your gifts and talents as zero. But, this may also be the story that provides you with the easiest way to cop out of taking responsibility for your life. If you have nothing to offer, you have nothing to do. If you have no utility at all, you have no responsibility. You don't need to learn to be productive. You don't need to learn how to love or care for someone. You don't even need to care for yourself.

TASK: Make a list of at least five times you catch yourself thinking or saying, "I have nothing to offer."

SESSION 3

EXERCISE 1C – EXPERIENCE SHARING, HANGING ON

Session 3 focuses your attention on stories you can have about the past that are undermining your ability to have a healthy and strong life. Let's get started.

Exercise 1 invites you to notice how often your stories include the theme, "I didn't have enough resources when I was growing up." You probably don't use the word "resources" in your story, but some other word like money, education, background, neighborhood, or friendships. The point of the story is that there was something lacking in the raw materials of your life that now makes it difficult, if not impossible, for you to succeed. While it is certainly true that some people are blessed with much more resource in their childhood than are others, it is not necessarily true that everyone who has more resource does better and all those who have lesser resource fail to achieve. Yet, the grip of this story can be strong and can limit the expectations you put on yourself to achieve.

TASK: Make a list of at least five times you catch yourself thinking or saying, "I didn't have enough resources when I was growing up."

EXERCISE 2C – EXPERIENCE SHARING, HANGING ON

Exercise 2 invites you to notice how often your stories include the theme, "I lacked the support I needed when I was growing up." Certainly, there is great value in having been raised by people who love and support you. There is no denying that having loving care givers is a great asset. But, the absence of that support is not a declaration of some lifelong handicap that cannot be overcome. Yet, it is easy for such a story to invite self-pity and excuse-making when things are challenging and difficult. Self-pity can undermine the very grit you need to keep moving forward.

TASK: Make a list of at least five times you catch yourself thinking or saying, "I lacked the support I needed when I was growing up."

EXERCISE 3C – EXPERIENCE SHARING, HANGING ON

Exercise 3 invites you to notice how often your stories include the theme, "Someone hurt me deeply and now I am scarred for life." People can do some very mean and vicious things to each other. Adults sometimes do very hurtful and evil things to small children. These are terrible wounds and they can be difficult to heal. But, they are even more destructive when they become the story of your life. This story can take such a strong hold on your life that everything becomes connected and related to the trauma you experienced. The traumas can then take over your whole life and leave no room for anything else.

TASK: Make a list of at least five times you catch yourself thinking or saying, "Someone hurt me deeply, and now I am scarred for life."

EXERCISE 4C – EXPERIENCE SHARING, HANGING ON

Exercise 4 invites you to notice how often your stories include the theme, "No one believed in me." There is much to be said for having someone in your life in your early years that encouraged you to dream big dreams and believed you could achieve them. Yet, for many people there were no such care givers. Instead, they were raised by people that had no dreams of their own and could offer none to their children. Some were diminished, criticized, and belittled by their parents. It may be more difficult to believe in yourself if you were not believed in, but it isn't impossible. When you are in the grip of the story that you can't have confidence in yourself because no one believed in you, you are trapped in insecurity and the sense of inadequacy.

TASK: Make a list of at least five times you catch yourself thinking or saying, "No one believed in me."

SESSION 4

EXERCISE 1D – EXPERIENCE SHARING, HANGING ON

Session 4 invites you to focus your attention on stories you might have about the future. The future is unknown to everyone, but the stories we create about the future shape how we face it and so influence our reaction. Let's get started.

Exercise 1 invites to you notice how often your stories include the theme, "The future is scary." Of course, bad things may (and likely, will) occur in your future, but the story that the future is scary sets you up to expect and prepare for it. Let's imagine you are taking a road trip tomorrow. Tonight, you are contemplating all that could go wrong. You could have a flat tire, run out of gas, break down, be carjacked, be robbed, get into an accident, or have a bridge collapse from under you. Any one of these could happen, but not one of them is likely to occur. But, the fear you can generate by thinking of them might actually talk you out of taking the trip. To the extent you create the story that "The future is scary," you will diminish your willingness to do anything new, unknown, or unpredictable.

TASK: Make a list of at least five times you catch yourself thinking or saying, "The future is scary."

EXERCISE 2D – EXPERIENCE SHARING, HANGING ON

Exercise 2 invites you to notice how often your stories include the theme, "The future is hopeless." The future is the unknown and unwritten part of your life. There is nothing you can do about the past; that part is already written. But, the future remains open to being shaped. When you cultivate the story that the future is hopeless, you will act as if you have no influence over what occurs.

Certainly, you don't control everything, but since you do control how you react, you have a fair amount of control as to how things go.

TASK: Make a list of at least five times you catch yourself thinking or saying, "The future is hopeless."

EXERCISE 3D – EXPERIENCE SHARING, HANGING ON

Exercise 3 invites you to notice how often your stories include the theme, "The future is determined by people other than me." This story is similar to the previous one, but with a twist. It sees others as having power while you do not. It tends to make people in positions of authority or privilege look like the ones in control of things, while you are at the effect of their choices. This story almost always leads to resentment, and resistance to people who are more powerful than are you. These people could be allies but for your story that gets in the way of forming such a relationship with them.

TASK: Make a list of at least five times when you catch yourself thinking or saying, "The future is determined by people other than me."

EXERCISE 4D – EXPERIENCE SHARING, HANGING ON

Exercise 4 invites you to notice how often your stories include the theme, "The future is already here." This story is built on the idea that there is nothing new coming your way. It is almost as if you have done all that you will ever do, and have all that you will ever have, so the future will be just like the present for the rest of your life. People who entertain this story don't dream of much or anything for their future. Because they don't dream, they don't plan to make new things happen. They make themselves content with the status quo, with what is. All striving and growing is surrendered. Their lives stagnate and gradually erode until there is little left.

TASK: Make a list of at least five times when you catch yourself thinking or saying, "My future is already here."

FACTOR – EXPERIENCE SHARING

The creation and telling of stories is part of the fabric of the human condition. Stories are no more than the meaning we make of the events in our lives. Our stories are, to some extent, always shaped by our past experiences and biases. We move toward Purpose when our stories inspire us to bring our best self into our work and lives, and when they support our understanding that our lives matter and that we can make a difference in the world. Our stories undermine our Purpose when they lead to bigotry, prejudice, selfishness, greed, envy, hatred, and all other attitudes that shrink our perspective and trap us in negativity and smallness.

SELF-ASSESSED RATING - ERODING

Your stories about yourself and the world often create drama that undermines your effectiveness.

SESSION 1

EXERCISE 1A – EXPERIENCE SHARING, ERODING

Your life is eroding, at least partly, due to how you deal with stories. We all make up stories about everything that happens in our lives. Stories are simply our interpretation of facts and include our biases, prejudices, and past experiences. Our stories can either support or undermine our ability to effectively relate to life. Rarely do we consider our stories and the impact they have on us. These exercises are designed to help you better understand that impact. Session 1 focuses your attention on understanding negative stories and how they might be impacting your life. Let's get started.

Exercise 1 invites you to see that any story that undermines your confidence in the goodness of life has a negative impact on you. Stories that cause you to worry about things that could happen to you and those you love are an excellent example. Mistrust in the goodness of life leads to anxiety, fear, and a reticence to embrace change as a positive force in your life. Yet it is easy to create such stories.

TASK: Make a list of at least five times you catch yourself creating a story that undermines your confidence in the goodness of life.

EXERCISE 2A – EXPERIENCE SHARING, ERODING

Exercise 2 invites you to see that any story you create that undermines your confidence in yourself has a significant negative impact on your life. When you think you aren't good enough to take on something new or feel insecure being who you are around others, you are in the grip of stories that undermine your confidence in yourself. They could show up at work when you turn down a new opportunity because you aren't certain you are up to it. They can show up in your social life when you avoid certain people because you don't feel good enough for them to accept you. Such negative stories cause you to hold back, to play a small game, and to limit your life in big and small ways.

TASK: Make a list of at least five times you catch yourself creating a story that undermines your confidence in yourself.

EXERCISE 3A – EXPERIENCE SHARING, ERODING

Exercise 3 invites you to see that any story you create that undermines your confidence in others has significant negative impact on your life. People are either an asset or a liability in your life. They are assets when you invite the people in your life to be your mentors, supporters, cheerleaders, coaches, guides, and friends. They are a liability when you view them as dangerous, scary, intimidating, rejecting, and hurtful. How you view the people in your life is almost entirely dependent on the stories you create about them. You may not always pay attention to the thoughts you create about the people in your life. Do you see your teachers as people who are rooting for your success and are eager to help you? Or, do you see them as guards and bullies who force you to do work you don't want to do and look for every opportunity to hold you back? If your stories support seeing them as people who want you to succeed, you are far more likely to seek their assistance than if you view them as out to get you.

TASK: Make a list of at least five times you catch yourself creating stories that undermine your confidence in the people in your life.

EXERCISE 4A – EXPERIENCE SHARING, ERODING

Exercise 4 invites you to see that any story you create that undermines your confidence in your future has significant impact on your life. The future is the unwritten part of your life. It will be whatever you make it to be. If you view the future with suspicion, as if it is stacked against you, or as if it is already set in stone, you have undermined your motivation to shape it. Why try if you can't succeed? You might be used to creating stories that people like you can't get ahead, or that your background doesn't qualify you to have a very successful life. Nothing could be further from the truth, but your stories are powerful enough to take all of the wind out of your sails.

TASK: Make a list of at least five times you catch yourself creating stories that undermine your confidence in the future.

SESSION 2

EXERCISE 1B – EXPERIENCE SHARING, ERODING

Session 2 focuses your attention on the value of positive stories. Positive stories foster the hope, confidence, and action you need to stop your life from eroding. Let's get started.

Exercise 1 invites you to see the value of creating positive stories about life. There are so many reasons to look at life from a positive point of view. Consider how much happens each day to support your life, with which you have nothing to do. The earth circles the sun, the rain falls, things grow. All of these are necessary to sustain you. Consider also that you have the amazing opportunity live, to experience, to love, to know, to learn. These realities can shape a wonderfully positive story, that life is an adventure that is wonderful and rich.

TASK: Write down a positive story about life.

EXERCISE 2B – EXPERIENCE SHARING, ERODING

Exercise 2 invites you to see the power of creating a positive story about yourself. When you look at your life through the lens of your natural gifts and talents, and the potential of what you can create, you open a world of new possibilities. This is a radical shift from the story that you aren't good enough. Consider the story that you have a unique gift that, when understood and utilized properly, will provide you with work that is enjoyable and earns you more than enough money for your life. What a wonderful story. When you hold a positive story about yourself, you are naturally motivated to discover your uniqueness and how it can be applied to the world around you.

TASK: Create a positive story about yourself. Write it down.

EXERCISE 3B – EXPERIENCE SHARING, ERODING

Exercise 3 invites you to see the power of creating a positive story about others. Take a few minutes and write down the names of the important people in your life. Now, consider the goodwill they have toward you. What dreams do they have for your life? What positive attributes do they see in you? How have they tried to assist you? When have they been there for you when you needed them? When you take the time to consider how valuable your friends and family are, you may discover an underutilized resource. Perhaps you can create a story that your boss wants you to succeed, and looks for opportunities to make you even more valuable at work. Stories that allow you to see the value of others are quite useful in opening your eyes to alliances and partnerships you may be overlooking.

TASK: Write down a positive story about the people in your life.

EXERCISE 4B – EXPERIENCE SHARING, ERODING

Exercise 4 invites you to see the power of creating a positive story about your future. Your story can be whatever you create. Regardless, it will have a very powerful influence on how you act and what you create for yourself. Take a few moments and consider the dreams you have for your life. You may realize that you rarely, if ever, consider your dreams and so nothing comes to mind. Having no dreams for the future makes it more likely that not much will happen in your future. Or, you may come to see that your dreams are quite modest. You only want your life to stop eroding. That isn't a bad dream, but you aren't asking for much. What if you had a wild dream; to have a life that is much better than the one you have? Does that dream have the power to help you create such a life?

TASK: Write down a positive dream for your future.

SESSION 3

EXERCISE 1C – EXPERIENCE SHARING, ERODING

Session 3 focuses your attention on how stories shape your life. Social science has long understood the interaction of beliefs, attitudes, and behavior. If any two of the three align, the third will follow along. Advertisers use this knowledge every day. If they want to sell you a certain laundry detergent, they will target all three factors. They try to influence your belief by showing you that their detergent gets your clothes cleaner than any other. They try to influence your attitude by showing you that beautiful and happy people use this detergent. Finally, they try to influence your behavior by putting the product on sale. They know that if they can get you to buy it, you will tend to believe it is the best product and will like it. If they can get you to believe in it and like it, you will buy it. Let's see how your stories work the same way.

Exercise 1 invites you to see that your stories, in many ways, create your beliefs. If someone cuts you off on the highway and you make up the story that it was intentional, you probably won't doubt that you are correct, even though you have no way of knowing if you are right or wrong. Your stories form almost all of your beliefs and, once they are in place, they are difficult to change.

TASK: See if you can identify five beliefs that you hold simply because you made up a story about something or someone.

EXERCISE 2C – EXPERIENCE SHARING, ERODING

Exercise 2 invites you to notice that your stories also influence your feeling or attitude toward the world around you. Let's take the story from the last exercise. You were cut off in traffic and immediately created the story that it was intentional. That belief spawns a feeling; anger. "How dare that person cut me off!" You might be able to feel anger even as you read this simply by imagining this happening to you. Notice, again, that you don't question the truth of your belief nor the validity of your reaction. Your anger may persist as you tell people about the person who intentionally cut you off.

TASK: See if you can identify five feelings or attitudes you have toward certain people or situations simply because you created a story about them.

EXERCISE 3C – EXPERIENCE SHARING, ERODING

Exercise 3 invites you to notice that your stories shape your behavior. Returning to your story about the person who you believe intentionally cut you off in traffic and toward whom you now have anger, you might find yourself wanting to race after them, honk your horn at them, or make some gesture to demonstrate your anger. Imagine how strange this behavior might seem to the person in the other car if they didn't intentionally cut you off, but simply didn't see you. You would look like a fool! But, when you are in the grip of your story, your behavior will follow along with whatever belief you have in your head. This example may be minor, but when your story impacts how you behave toward your best friend, your spouse, your boss, or someone of a different race or religion from you, it can have very serious implications for your life.

TASK: Make a list of at least five times your behavior was guided by some story you had in your head.

EXERCISE 4C – EXPERIENCE SHARING, ERODING

Exercise 4 invites you to notice how your stories can lead to patterns of behavior that can explain why your life is eroding. Your life is not what it could be because too many of your stories are out of alignment with the opportunities you are being provided. Your stories either limit your ability to see the opportunity, to understand it as an opportunity, your confidence in your ability to seize the opportunity, or your ability to succeed in that opportunity. Until you can see these stories clearly and understand them as only stories, you will remain in their grip and be unable to shift to a place where you can grow and thrive.

TASK: Make a list of at least five stories you have that limit your ability to stabilize your life.

SESSION 4

EXERCISE 1D – EXPERIENCE SHARING, ERODING

Session 4 focuses your attention on how you can loosen the grip of stories that are undermining your ability to build a stable and successful life. Let's get started.

Exercise 1 invites you to identify whatever stories are currently getting in your way. Take the time to do an honest assessment of your life. Where are things not working? Perhaps it is at work where you keep getting into some kind of trouble. Or, perhaps it is a home where you continually get into silly arguments that undermine the stability and peace of your home.

TASK: Pick the area of your life that most needs to be addressed. Once you have done so, write down every story you have about that person, situation, or place. Write out your stories completely.

EXERCISE 2D – EXPERIENCE SHARING, ERODING

Exercise 2 invites you to identify who you become inside of the context of the stories you wrote down in Exercise 1. Notice that your stories create a context that determines what you believe, how you feel, and what you do. You take on an identity or role in response to your story. If your story is that your boss is a bully, you might become the victim. You think like a victim, feel like a victim, and act like a victim. If your story is that your spouse is lazy, you might become the disciplinarian. You believe it is necessary for you to take that role and you take it on.

TASK: Write down who you become in the context of your stories from Exercise 1.

EXERCISE 3D – EXPERIENCE SHARING, ERODING

Exercise 3 invites you to create new stories. Remember that your stories are just stories. They aren't true, and since that is the case, you can create different stories. They, too, won't be true, but they will create a new context; one in which you can take on a different, and perhaps more functional, role. Create a new story about your boss. He isn't a bully; he is under a lot of pressure to succeed and needs your help. Create a new story about your spouse. He isn't lazy. He is worn out from how hard he works. These new stories act as new lenses through which you see the other person. And with the new story, you will have new feelings and behaviors.

TASK: Create new stories for all of the stories you wrote down in Exercise 1.

EXERCISE 4D – EXPERIENCE SHARING, ERODING

Exercise 4 invites you to take on a new role inside of the context of your new stories. Since you no longer see your boss as a bully, but as someone who needs help, you can decide to be the one who offers assistance. Since you no longer see your spouse as lazy, but tired, you can decide to stop being the disciplinarian and instead, offer rest and refreshment. You can become a whole new person in the relationship; someone who shows up very differently. In doing so, you can reverse old patterns that have kept your life in decline.

TASK: Decide who you will be in each of your new stories. Once you have done so, consciously demonstrate your new self every day.

FACTOR – EXPERIENCE SHARING

The creation and telling of stories is part of the fabric of the human condition. Stories are no more than the meaning we make of the events in our lives. Our stories are, to some extent, always shaped by our past experiences and biases. We move toward Purpose when our stories inspire us to bring our best self into our work and lives, and when they support our understanding that our lives matter and that we can make a difference in the world. Our stories undermine our Purpose when they lead to bigotry, prejudice, selfishness, greed, envy, hatred, and all other attitudes that shrink our perspective and trap us in negativity and smallness.

SELF-ASSESSED RATING - TREADING WATER

Your stories about yourself and the world tend to be supportive, but don't challenge you to find your greatness.

SESSION 1

EXERCISE 1A – EXPERIENCE SHARING, TREADING WATER

You are treading water because of your mixed relationship with the stories you tell yourself. They are sufficient for you to create a stable and secure life, but not adequate to inspire you to grow and thrive. These exercises are designed to help you better understand the role stories play in the construction of your life, how they are impacting you, and how you might change your stories to move you beyond treading water. Session 1 focuses your attention on better understanding the power of stories. Let's get started.

Exercise 1 invites you to see that you create stories about everything. This is such a natural and normal process that you may not often stop to consider how frequently you engage in story making and telling. Stories are simply your interpretation of whatever is happening in your life. And, literally nothing happens without you making it into a story. You see each event through your history and experience, your successes and failures, and your fears and desires.

TASK: Make a list of at least five things that have occurred today. Now, write down the story you created about each one. For example, the barista didn't respond when you ordered coffee. The story you made up is that he is new at his job and doesn't yet know how to attend to customers.

EXERCISE 2A – EXPERIENCE SHARING, TREADING WATER

Exercise 2 invites you to notice that you tend to believe your stories are true. Now that you notice how often you create stories, it is important to become aware of how quickly and thoroughly you believe the stories you just made up are true. It is as natural as breathing. When you say to yourself that the barista is new, you take that to be a fact, even though you have no earthly idea if he just got the job or has been working there for 20 years. You don't question your commitment to your story. You might quickly see the danger here. Since stories just pop into your head whenever anything happens, and since they are the result of all of the experiences you have had in the past, the chance that they are accurate is not high. You are much more likely to be wrong than to be right. And, it is these stories that are guiding your life.

TASK: Review your list of stories. Notice how committed you are to them being true.

EXERCISE 3A – EXPERIENCE SHARING, TREADING WATER

Exercise 3 invites you to notice that your stories become filters through which you live your life. Now that you see how quickly you adopt your stories, not as stories but as truth, it is good to become aware of how those stories begin to shape your life. You now see, feel, and act through the lens of your story. Since you are convinced the barista is new, you feel sorry for him and give him a bigger tip because you know how difficult it is to get everything right when you start a new job. Or, you might have a different reaction. Since he didn't pay attention to you, you find yourself angry at management for putting someone so new and poorly trained in such an important role. All of this, regardless of how you react, is totally driven by your story. Even though your story might be completely wrong, you are living, breathing, acting, and reacting based upon it. Imagine all of the damage you might be doing by riding off on your story-horse that is only a figment of your imagination.

TASK: Make a list of five mistakes you have made because of your stories. You might have been angry at someone for something they didn't do, but you couldn't see it because of your story. Or, you might have fallen in love with someone who was no good, but your story didn't allow you to see it. Wow!

EXERCISE 4A – EXPERIENCE SHARING, TREADING WATER

Exercise 4 invites you to notice that you often cling to your stories. We become so attached to our stories that we often try to cling to them even when faced with information that negates them. In fact, most of our prejudices and biases are demonstrations of this truth. Your experience with the barista has now tainted your view of Starbucks. You won't ever go into one of their stores. Not only that, but you find yourself trying to convince all of your friends to boycott the stores because of how you were treated. When your friends disagree with you, you find yourself becoming animated (and even angry), protesting that they don't understand. You won't even listen to another opinion. You are in the grip of your story and you can't break free. We have all had times when we found ourselves so tightly controlled by our story that we can't seem to break its hold. It could be some grudge you have been nursing for years. Or, it could be some hurt from the past you can't release.

TASK: Make a list of at least five stories you have clung to. Perhaps you are in the grip of some now.

SESSION 2

EXERCISE 1B – EXPERIENCE SHARING, TREADING WATER

Session 2 focuses your attention on stories you might have that allow you to tread water. You might not have the exact story we mention, but may have one that is similar. Let's get started.

Session 1 invites you to notice that you have a story about life that goes something like this: "My life is meant to be okay. Not great, but certainly not bad." Everyone has standards of what they expect from life. You may not realize how much that standard determines what will happen in your life. Your story is that your life is meant to be stable and secure. This is a tremendously valuable story to have. When bad things happen to you, some bell rings in your head and you get to work solving the problem and restoring your wellbeing. You simply won't allow bad things to undermine your life. Not everyone has a story that allows their life to respond to crisis this way. Your story motives you to create order in your life; to do things that will allow you to have a stable career and family and solid friendships.

TASK: Write down your story about life.

EXERCISE 2B – EXPERIENCE SHARING, TREADING WATER

Exercise 2 invites you to notice the story you have about yourself. It is likely that your story about yourself goes something like this: "I am basically a good and average person." Again, this is a very positive story to have. You don't see yourself as weak or ineffective. You don't think you need others to take care of you. You see yourself as capable. You set reasonable expectations for yourself that you are able to achieve. You fit in almost everywhere you go. You enjoy yourself and your life. This is the story of someone who is treading water. It is a little like vanilla ice cream; everyone likes you but you don't stand out.

TASK: Write your story about yourself. See if you can capture the essence of what you believe about yourself.

EXERCISE 3B – EXPERIENCE SHARING, TREADING WATER

Exercise 3 invites you to notice the story you have about people. Your story about people is likely to be that they are basically good and well-intentioned. This story allows you to interact with people in a positive and meaningful way. You don't expect everyone you meet to try to hurt or cheat you. You don't tend to harbor grudges or carry wounds from the past. You find people interesting to be around and know how to converse and relate in a way that is comfortable and easy.

People generally like you because you like them. This makes you easy to be around at work, at home, and in your neighborhood.

TASK: Write down your story about people. See if you can list some outcomes of your story and how they have benefitted your life.

EXERCISE 4B – EXPERIENCE SHARING, TREADING WATER

Exercise 4 invites you to see the story you have about your past. Your story is likely to be that the past is the past. You see your upbringing as reasonably positive. Of course, some bad things happened, but you don't dwell on them. Your story is that you had a happy childhood that prepared you well to be an adult. As a result of that story you don't dwell on the past. You don't carry a sense of injustice for not being treated well. You don't see yourself as flawed in some way. Your story about the past allows you to extract the goodness from your history, and to use it for the foundation of your life. You model your family interactions after those of your family of origin. You carry forward many of the family rituals and patterns of your childhood.

TASK: Write down your story about your past. Can you see how your story allows you to leave behind the negative and to move the positive forward into your life?

SESSION 3

EXERCISE 1C – EXPERIENCE SHARING, TREADING WATER

Session 3 focuses your attention on stories that might be holding you back from growing. Self-limiting stories are not uncommon. In fact, we imagine almost everyone has a few. Understanding them and their impact is key to getting beyond their influence. Let's get started.

Exercise 1 invites you to notice stories you have about life that cause you to settle for less than you could have. Such stories come in many flavors but share one theme: life is good enough as it is. You might have a story that your life is better than you expected, and so it is enough. Or, you could have a story that you have just been lucky and don't deserve more. Or, you could have a story that having more would require too much of you. All such stories create the same result; they encourage you to be content rather than pressing ahead for more. They limit your ability to imagine you could have more love, wealth, success, popularity, impact, or whatever "more" you might otherwise want. It is such stories about life that will stall your growth and development.

TASK: See if you can list five stories you have about life that are currently limiting your growth.

EXERCISE 2C – EXPERIENCE SHARING, TREADING WATER

Exercise 2 invites you to notice how your stories about yourself can limit your life. While you might think you are a good person, your story might not include those things about you that are truly remarkable and special. And while it might be true that, in some ways, you are ordinary, it is also true that in some ways you are extraordinary. But, your story about yourself might not have room to see yourself in so beautiful a way. Your story might label such things as boasting, flaunting, or self-centeredness. If that is the case, your story won't allow you to see the very gifts that you need to embrace and utilize to get to the next level of your life. It is only when you embrace your voice that you will sing from your soul. It is only when you embrace your creativity that your art will shine.

TASK: See if you can list five stories you have about yourself being ordinary that limit your ability to see, and to embrace, what is extraordinary about you.

EXERCISE 3C – EXPERIENCE SHARING, TREADING WATER

Exercise 3 invites you to notice how your stories about others can limit your life. While you generally have positive stories toward the people in your life, you might notice that those same stories don't include inspiring, encouraging, and pressing others to live up to their greatness. Your stories make it easy for you to relate in an easeful manner. You are comfortable with small talk, passing the time, and creating mutually good feelings. Your stories may not require you to seek that which is the very best in your coworkers, family, and friends because, if you don't require more of them, they won't require more of you. Stories that don't press others to do, give, and be more tend to foster mediocrity.

TASK: Make a list of at least five stories you have toward others that inhibit demanding more of them (and of you).

EXERCISE 4C – EXPERIENCE SHARING, TREADING WATER

Exercise 4 invites you to notice your stories about your future and how they shape your life. Your future is yet to be written. Your stories will dramatically shape what you write. If they are big and ambitious stories, your life might dramatically change as you move into your future. If your stories are modest and conservative, you may not change much at all. Notice what you tell yourself about your future. If you feel you have accomplished much of what you will accomplish, you will not seek many new adventures. If you tell yourself that you have many mountains to climb and things still to do, it really doesn't matter what your age is. You will continue to have ever-expanding adventures. Your stories are shaping your future as you read these words, whether or not you realize it.

TASK: Make a list of at least five stories you have about your future, and consider how they are shaping your choices.

SESSION 4

EXERCISE 1D – EXPERIENCE SHARING, TREADING WATER

Session 4 focuses your attention on some ways you can strengthen your stories, so as to support moving beyond treading water and toward growing. Let's get started.

Exercise 1 invites you to notice your stories and how they are impacting your life. Many people are completely unaware of how much their lives are shaped by their stories. Simply noticing the influence of your stories breaks their grip. By noticing, you acknowledge that whatever you are thinking, feeling, and doing may be as much a reaction to something made up as it is to what is truly occurring. This allows you to have some uncertainty and so to emotionally separate a bit from whatever you are planning to do.

TASK: You can practice this by noticing your stories as you go through the day, and labeling them as stories. You had a story about the barista. You had a story about the person who cut you off. You really don't know much about either of them. So, your reaction may not be appropriate.

EXERCISE 2D – EXPERIENCE SHARING, TREADING WATER

Exercise 2 invites you to hold your stories lightly. Practice creating alternative stories that would explain the same facts. The barista could be having trouble at home, or might have a hearing issue, or might be suffering from student debt. Any of these could explain why he is distracted. Be creative. Generate as many alternative stories as you can and notice how they loosen the tightness of the grip of your first story. You begin to relax and to entertain alternative reactions. You have the space to breathe, to ask questions, and to make more rational and reasonable decisions.

TASK: Practice generating alternative stories at least three times each day for the next week.

EXERCISE 3D – EXPERIENCE SHARING, TREADING WATER

Exercise 3 invites you to generate positive stories for your life. Stories are the opportunity for you to be creative in a way that can change your life in dramatic ways. Consider the story that you have an amazing talent that has not yet been discovered. Such a story sets you on a journey to uncover your unique skill. Or, consider the story that you could be making twice the income you are making now. That story sets you on the quest for a new and very different job. You can create stories about life, yourself, the people in your world, and your future that challenge you to move beyond treading water and to grow.

TASK: Make a list of 10 stories you could make up about yourself that would inspire you to achieve bigger and better things.

EXERCISE 4D – EXPERIENCE SHARING, TREADING WATER

Exercise 4 invites you to put your new stories into action. You do this by deciding who you will be in the context of your new story. For example, if you make up the story that you have an amazing and undiscovered talent, you can decide you are the one responsible to uncover it. That is who you will be. So, each day decide what you will do to discover that hidden talent. If you create the story that you will make twice your current income, decide who you will be to make that happen. You will be a job seeker of a dramatically different opportunity. What will you do today to make that dream come true? Begin acting that part. By putting your stories into action, you can dramatically change your life.

TASK: Take one of your dreams from the last exercise and write down five ways you can put it into practice. Now do those things each day for the next week.

FACTOR – EXPERIENCE SHARING

The creation and telling of stories is part of the fabric of the human condition. Stories are no more than the meaning we make of the events in our lives. Our stories are, to some extent, always shaped by our past experiences and biases. We move toward Purpose when our stories inspire us to bring our best self into our work and lives, and when they support our understanding that our lives matter and that we can make a difference in the world. Our stories undermine our Purpose when they lead to bigotry, prejudice, selfishness, greed, envy, hatred, and all other attitudes that shrink our perspective and trap us in negativity and smallness.

SELF-ASSESSED RATING - GROWING

Your stories about yourself and the world are positive, and they challenge you to grow and expand.

SESSION 1

EXERCISE 1A – EXPERIENCE SHARING, GROWING

Your life is growing, at least partly, because most of your "stories" support your success. The purpose of these exercises is to assist you in understanding the power of stories in shaping your life, understanding where your stories might be keeping you from fully thriving, and giving you the skills to move beyond whatever limitations they may be imposing on your life. Session 1 focuses your attention on how stories operate. Let's get started.

Exercise 1 invites you to see that you create stories about everything. This is such a natural and normal process that you may not often stop to consider how frequently you engage in story making and telling. Stories are simply your interpretation of whatever is happening in your life. And, literally nothing happens without you making it into a story. You see each event that occurs through your history and experience, your successes and failures, and your fears and desires.

TASK: Notice how often you create stories today. Keep a list until you become aware that you would be writing down almost everything.

EXERCISE 2A – EXPERIENCE SHARING, GROWING

Exercise 2 invites you to see how stories can support your success. When your stories inspire and motivate you to believe you can continue to take on new challenges and have exciting adventures, they are extremely valuable. If you create the story that the vacation you are considering, to travel through Italy taking cooking lessons from fabulous chefs, will be a terrific way for you to expand your culinary skills, you are quite likely to sign up and plan your trip. Your life is filled with stories such as this; expectations that the future would be bright and that you had what it took to learn something new or to try something different. Such stories have been a key to your success.

TASK: Make a list of at least five positive stories that have supported your growth as a person.

EXERCISE 3A – EXPERIENCE SHARING, GROWING

Exercise 3 invites you to see that your stories can also hold you back. If you are considering that same trip to Italy and create the story that the kitchens will be hot, the tasks they give you will be laborious, the language barrier will be difficult, and you might be kidnapped by terrorists, you are far more likely to pick something else to do that sounds easier and safer. This is how stories can hold you back from thriving. When they induce unnecessary fear or undermine your confidence, they can rob you of the motivation to take on something new or to tackle an interesting opportunity.

TASK: See if you can list five stories you have created that have robbed you of something you were considering doing.

EXERCISE 4A – EXPERIENCE SHARING, GROWING

Exercise 4 invites you to see that your stories are completely under your control. You can't control the stories that pop into your head, but you can control how much they affect your choices. You do this by generating alternative stories that weaken your conviction in the story you first created. If you initially generated the story that your anticipated Italian cooking adventure was going to be difficult and dangerous, you might notice that story and then consider alternatives. You might ask yourself how you know it will be difficult and dangerous. You might consider that other people have taken this same vacation and have written positive things about it. You might remind yourself of how much you like Italian food and that you would enjoy learning to cook it more authentically. You might remember times when you figured out how to communicate with someone who spoke a different language, and how much fun you had overcoming that barrier. These new stories can alter your perspective on the trip so you can make a more reasoned decision.

TASK: Think of one story that might currently be holding you back, and write down at least 10 alternative stories. See how it impacts your thoughts, feelings, and considerations.

SESSION 2

EXERCISE 1B – EXPERIENCE SHARING, GROWING

Session 2 focuses your attention on some of the stories that foster a life that is growing but not yet thriving. Perhaps you will be able to see yourself in some of these stories. Let's get started.

Exercise 1 invites you consider the story that goes something like this: "I am better than average, but not exceptional." This seems like a reasonable story, doesn't it? It supports extending the effort to distinguish you from most people by working harder, setting bigger goals, creating more success, and having a richer life. Yet, it does not support being exceptional. That story doesn't allow you to see what is truly unique and what would distinguish you from everyone else. Hence, as long as you are in the grip of this story, it will be difficult to fully thrive.

TASK: Write down your variation of this story.

EXERCISE 2B – EXPERIENCE SHARING, GROWING

Exercise 2 invites you to consider the story that goes something like this: "I can have what I want but with limitation." Again, this is a reasonable story. It allows you to dream reasonably big dreams and to expand your life in meaningful ways. You can have a similar story and have a very successful life. You will have a good marriage, a happy family, and a successful career. But, what if there is more that you haven't even considered and would not ever begin to consider, if your story imposes limitations? Such a story imposes such a blind spot. It will not allow you to dream without constraints, or to throw open all possibilities for what you can want, do, and be.

TASK: Write down your variation of this story.

EXERCISE 3B – EXPERIENCE SHARING, GROWING

Exercise 3 invites you to consider the story that goes something like this: "Everything should be done in moderation." This is good advice. Many things taken to the extreme become harmful. Being in balance certainly has its merits. This story will make sure you color within the lines, and are seen as a good person who is always appropriate and respectful. But, this story can make it difficult for you to embrace and live in your uniqueness. Thriving often requires a degree of imbalance or, perhaps better said, "unique balance." A great painter may paint through the night when inspired. A great writer might sequester herself away for weeks while working on her novel. An inspired business person might keep his team focused for days on creating a breakthrough idea.

TASK: Write down your version of the story, "Everything should be done in moderation." How is that story constraining your thriving?

EXERCISE 4B – EXPERIENCE SHARING, GROWING

Exercise 4 invites you to consider the story that goes something like this: "It is important for me to fit in." Fitting in is a very important skill to have. It allows you to interact with people in an effective manner. It provides you with social connections and necessary alliances. But, this story creates its own constraints. Sometimes the cost of fitting in is the denial of what is most special about you. Please notice that many of the great men and women in history didn't always fit in. Instead, they often went against the grain. They were often rejected, misunderstood, and even persecuted. How can you fully thrive unless you are willing to be all of your uniqueness and are willing to pay whatever price that requires?

TASK: Write down your version of the story, "It is important to fit in."

SESSION 3

EXERCISE 1C – EXPERIENCE SHARING, GROWING

Session 3 focuses your attention on the type of stories that support thriving. Let's get started.

Exercise 1 invites you to consider the story that goes something like this: "I can have whatever I want." This might sound like a dangerous story as it could lead to unrealistic expectations, disappointment and/or aberrant behavior. Perhaps it could, but such a story might also empower you to dream very big dreams and to take on very big challenges. When President John F. Kennedy challenged the U.S. to put a man on the moon it sounded absolutely impossible. And, then it was done. Thriving requires dreaming without limits. It is only this kind of thinking that can bring out the very best in a person. When you believe you can have anything, or do anything, a world of new possibilities open. If that is so, what will you do?

TASK: See if you can write down a story that expresses your version of "I can have anything."

EXERCISE 2C – EXPERIENCE SHARING, GROWING

Exercise 2 invites you to consider the story that goes something like this: "I can be extraordinary." It might be easy to see the ways you are ordinary. Every day you brush your teeth, get dressed, and eat breakfast pretty much like everyone else. Nothing about that seems extraordinary. And, certainly there are many things about you and your life that may be ordinary. But, only a story like this one can empower you to seek what is truly extraordinary about you. Gandhi was a little man and an average attorney. It was only when he discovered that he could be extraordinary that he became the man who would change the world. Steve Jobs could be nasty and overbearing with people, but his vision for the Macintosh computer was truly extraordinary. It is only when you believe that extraordinary lives within you that you will dare to search for it and show it to the world.

TASK: See if you can write down your version of the story that you are extraordinary.

EXERCISE 3C – EXPERIENCE SHARING, GROWING

Exercise 3 invites you to consider the story that goes something like this: "Life is an endless adventure." Life is different for each of us. For some, it is something to endure. For others, it is a constant headache. For others, it is a struggle. Is it life that is those things, or is it our story about life that shapes our experience? What if you tried on the story of life being an endless adventure? What might you choose to do? What adventure might you take? Would you take a river boat up the Yangtze River, swim in the Amazon, or climb Mount McKinley? Or, you might choose to fall wildly in love, go back to school, or start the new career you had always dreamed about. Thinking of life as a constant adventure might entice you to shake off mediocrity and boredom to take on something new and different.

TASK: See if you can write down your version of the story that life is an endless adventure.

EXERCISE 4C – EXPERIENCE SHARING, GROWING

Exercise 4 invites you to consider the story that goes something like this: "I don't need to worry about getting hurt." So much of life is organized around avoiding getting hurt. You won't try something new because you don't want to fail. You don't say what you think because you fear being criticized. You don't wear what you want because you don't want to be laughed at. You don't do what you want because you don't want to be excluded. You don't go on great adventures because you don't want...What if you substituted your story with "I don't need to worry about getting hurt"? You could be completely free and fearless. You could be unconstrained and bold. You could take risks. Thriving requires being fearless. You become fearless when you give up worry about getting hurt and value your self-expression higher than safety. If you get hurt, you will heal. If you don't take the risk you may miss the adventure of your life.

TASK: See if you can write down your version of the story that "I don't need to worry about getting hurt."

SESSION 4

EXERCISE 1D – EXPERIENCE SHARING, GROWING

Session 4 focuses your attention on how you can shift your stories from ones that support your growth to ones that support your thriving. Let's get started.

Exercise 1 invites you to be vigilant about your stories and how they shape your life. Hopefully, these exercises have made you more aware of your stories and the impact they have on your beliefs, attitudes, and behavior. Now, we ask you to begin noticing your stories. What are you saying to yourself about life, yourself, the people you know, and about your future? Which of those stories supports your thriving and which ones hold you back?

TASK: Begin keeping two lists and adding to them daily. Notice how those stories that are holding you back are influencing your decisions. The more clearly you see your stories and their impact, the more control you will have over them.

EXERCISE 2D – EXPERIENCE SHARING, GROWING

Exercise 2 invites you to practice creating new, more productive stories. Wherever you find yourself creating stories that are holding you back from thriving, create a new story that breaks through that barrier. Suppose you find yourself creating the story that you shouldn't travel overseas because the danger of terrorism is too high. You find yourself fearful and reluctant to travel. Create a new story that the value of adventure and what you might learn and experience is worth too much to give up to any threat. Your new story will empower you to continue to take risks and to grow.

TASK: This week practice creating new stories for every story that is holding you back. Notice the impact on your choices.

EXERCISE 3D – EXPERIENCE SHARING, GROWING

Exercise 3 invites you to practice redefining yourself inside of the context of your new stories. Your old stories resulted in you being fearful, or cautious, or careful. Your new story allows you to be bold, fearless, and expansive. Defining who you are in light of your new story allows you to take on a new way of being in the world, one that presents you with new opportunities to grow and express yourself more fully.

TASK: This week practice writing down who you will be in light of your new stories. Be clear as to how what you will believe, what you will feel, and how you will act.

EXERCISE 4D – EXPERIENCE SHARING, GROWING

Exercise 4 invites you to put your new self into play in your life. Every day you can practice being the person you decided to be in the context of your new story about life. This is more powerful than you can imagine.

TASK: If you decided to be fearless, practice not responding to threat by cowering or holding back. If you decided to be an adventurer, practice taking adventures. If you decided to love boldly, give yourself fully to someone you love. The more you practice deciding who you will be and then being that person, the more you will control your destiny and create a life that is thriving. Start today.

EXERCISE SERIES: SELF-DECEPTION

FACTOR – SELF-DECEPTION

Only if we possess the ability to be honest with ourselves can we cultivate our true purpose.

SELF-ASSESSED RATING - HANGING ON

You maintain a self-serving view of yourself and your life that is filled with distortion and undermines your ability to make constructive choices.

SESSION 1

EXERCISE 1A – SELF-DECEPTION, HANGING ON

One of the reasons you are hanging on by your fingernails is the degree to which you suffer from self-deception. Self-deception is the choice to fool yourself about what is going on around you. The greater your self-deception, the greater the difficulty in effectively relating to life. Because you aren't seeing things accurately, the decisions you make are not likely to be helpful. These exercises are designed to help you understand how self-deception might be showing up in your life and the damage it is doing. Session 1 focuses your attention on self-deception about your past. Let's get started.

Exercise 1 invites you to see that you can fool yourself about how good your past was. You may overlook patterns of behavior that were quite unhealthy or even destructive by telling yourself that you had a normal upbringing and that everyone has those same experiences in their past. You may have grown up around people who didn't know how to resolve conflict in a constructive manner and so screamed and yelled at each other. Because you fool yourself about this dysfunctional behavior, you make it easy to carry it forward into your current family and friendships. Instead of making different choices, you perpetuate problems that need to be fixed.

TASK: Make a list of five dysfunctions from your past that you have been treating as if they were normal.

EXERCISE 2A – SELF-DECEPTION, HANGING ON

Exercise 2 invites you to see that you can fool yourself about how bad the past was. Self-deception can move in the very opposite direction from what we considered in Exercise 1. You can make the mistake of exaggerating the dysfunctions from your past such that you act as if they are still occurring in your life, and you continue to be at the effect of something that happened years ago. When you make this mistake, you fail to move past your old circumstances. You were teased as a child and now make it a point of telling everyone how damaged you were by teasing. You continue to be overly sensitive to any kind of joking and react to even mild ribbing as if you are still a small child. Such self-deception makes it almost impossible to mature and grow.

TASK: Make a list of five dysfunctions from your past that you exaggerate and/or hold on to.

EXERCISE 3A – SELF-DECEPTION, HANGING ON

Exercise 3 invites you to see that you can fool yourself about past failures. This self-deception perpetuates times when things didn't work out as you wanted or expected by generalizing the failure until it impacts almost every area of your life. You were fired from your job without any notice or warning. It caught you completely by surprise. You felt like a failure. Now, you live in constant fear of being fired. You are unwilling to take any risks at work like asking for a promotion or a new job because you worry it will put you at greater risk of being fired. The threat of repeating your failure has backed you into a corner that makes it very difficult to grow and succeed.

TASK: Make a list of five past failures that you may be making too big and to which you are giving too much power.

EXERCISE 4A – SELF-DECEPTION, HANGING ON

Exercise 4 invites you to see that you can fool yourself about past fears and traumas. This self-deception expands fears and traumas such that they dominate your life and create emotional paralysis. Bad things happen. If you can let them go, you can learn and keep moving forward. When you hold on to them and let them grow, they can radically limit your life. When you were young, you were bitten by a dog. It wasn't that serious of a bite but you were very frightened, and you haven't let it go. You are now afraid of all dogs. You are unwilling to take a walk because you might encounter a dog. You not only are fearful of dogs, but your fear has now grown to include other animals. Your self-deception is making you housebound.

TASK: Make a list of five fears or traumas you have exaggerated and/or held onto.

SESSION 2

EXERCISE 1B – SELF-DECEPTION, HANGING ON

In addition to self-deception about your past, you can also deceive yourself about yourself. When you fall prey to these distortions you don't see yourself as others see you. This invariably leads to missteps and problems. Session 2 focuses your attention on ways you might be deceiving yourself about who you are. Let's get started.

Exercise 1 invites you to notice that you may be distorting your view of your talent. Perhaps you have known someone who strongly believed they had a beautiful singing voice when, in truth, they couldn't carry a tune. Even though everyone knew they couldn't sing, they wouldn't face it themselves. Hence, they kept trying out for various choirs and talent shows only to be consistently rejected. You may also have the opposite distortion about your talent; viewing yourself as lacking talents that you truly possess. In this case, you won't take advantage of opportunities where you could easily succeed because you refuse to acknowledge your abilities.

TASK: See if you can list any self-deception in your talent. If you need help, ask a few friends for feedback.

EXERCISE 2B – SELF-DECEPTION, HANGING ON

Exercise 2 invites you to see that you can fool yourself about your value. You may either view yourself as being more or less important than you truly are. If you have too lofty a view of yourself, you come across to others as a snob, self-absorbed, or egotistical. If you view yourself as less important that you are, you see others as weak, ineffective, and invisible. Either distortion will undermine the effectiveness of your life and make it very difficult to relate to others in a meaningful way.

TASK: See if you can list some ways you deceive yourself about your value.

EXERCISE 3B – SELF-DECEPTION, HANGING ON

Exercise 3 invites you to see that you can fool yourself about your success. Perhaps you have known someone who takes credit for work she did not do; claiming a much bigger share of responsibility than she earned. It isn't that she is lying. She actually thinks the credit belongs to her. That is the self-deception. Taking credit you don't deserve leads to resentment from those who actually did the work. It also creates a problem when you believe you can do things you don't actually possess the skills to do because you can't see the credit that properly belongs to you.

TASK: See if you can list any instances where you have taken credit for something you did not do.

EXERCISE 4B – SELF-DECEPTION, HANGING ON

Exercise 4 invites you to see that you can fool yourself about your limitations. People who fall prey to this distortion sometimes believe they can do anything they put their mind to. They come across as cocky and full of themselves. They fail to see their weaknesses and needs accurately. Sometimes this distortion leads to great danger when you put yourself in a place where you are way over your head. You might believe you can swim across the lake, until you are halfway across and find you are running out of gas. You might take on a job that requires skills you simply don't possess. Mistakes of this sort consistently lead to failure and make it very difficult to build a record of steady success.

TASK: See if you can list times when you failed to accurately assess your limitations.

SESSION 3

EXERCISE 1C – SELF-DECEPTION, HANGING ON

Session 3 focuses your attention on self-distortion about life. In many ways life is what you make it to be. Strong biases that limit your ability to see life's opportunities consistently create problems. Let's get started.

Exercise 1 invites you to notice the self-deception that life owes you something. Distortions of this type lead to a sense of entitlement. Perhaps you know someone who doesn't think he needs to work because the government owes him. Or, your spouse might feel entitled to do nothing when he gets home because he worked so hard. You can have entitlements toward your children that they owe you love, respect, or obedience. As you might imagine, entitlements lead to problems because others don't agree that you are entitled. When they don't give you what you expect, it is easy for conflict to occur.

TASK: List at least five of your entitlements.

EXERCISE 2C – SELF-DECEPTION, HANGING ON

Exercise 2 invites you to notice the self-deception in the belief that life is against you. When you fool yourself into thinking life is against you, it seems almost impossible to get ahead. All you see are obstacles. You can't see that anyone wants to help you. You might not apply for the new job because you know you won't get it. At least that is what you tell yourself. You view the whole world as if the deck is stacked against you. Perhaps you know someone with this self-deception and you have grown tired of their complaints about their life and their excuses why nothing positive will work out for them. And, perhaps you sometimes fall into that same trap.

TASK: See if you can notice yourself using language that suggests you see life as being against you.

EXERCISE 3C – SELF-DECEPTION, HANGING ON

Exercise 3 invites you to notice the self-deception in the belief that life isn't fair. This is a similar theme to life being against you, but is not quite so toxic. It isn't that life is against you, but that the rules of life are unpredictable and capricious. Hence, it is difficult to invest a lot of effort to try to create good things when you have no idea if you will get a return on your investment. When you are in the grip of this distortion, it is easy to talk yourself out of things by saying, "What's the use? Why go to school and do all of that work? It won't lead to a new opportunity." Or, "What's the use in losing weight? No one will ask me out." This distortion robs you of the motivation to make positive change.

TASK: See if you can list three ways you fool yourself by saying that life isn't fair.

EXERCISE 4C – SELF-DECEPTION, HANGING ON

Exercise 4 invites you to notice the self-deception in the belief that life is too hard. This too, is a very negative and disempowering distortion about life. Clearly, life is a struggle. Every breath you take requires effort. Nothing is accomplished by anyone without taking risks and applying talent to opportunity. The belief that life is too hard sets you up to not even try. There are amazing stories about servicemen and women who come from war without limbs but don't have any notion that life is too hard. It is just different. There are new challenges to face. But, many who have no disability other than self-deception come to believe that regardless of how hard they try and what they do, it is of no use. Life is simply too hard for them to get to a good place. So, they don't try. They coast. They let their lives fall into disrepair. They become less useful and are left further behind with the passage of time.

TASK: See if you can list five ways you tell yourself that life is too hard to be worth the effort.

SESSION 4

EXERCISE 1D – SELF-DECEPTION, HANGING ON

Session 4 focuses your attention on some things you can do to move beyond the self-deception that undermines your life. Let's get started.

Exercise 1 invites you to take a very first step by looking for your self-deception. By definition, this is a very difficult thing to do because you are deceiving yourself in these areas. But, if the previous exercises were useful to you in any way, they may have begun to open your eyes to some of the ways you have been fooling yourself. If you can't see your self-deception, you are in its control. If you can see it, if only a little, you can begin to manage it.

TASK: A good habit is to keep a diary in which you record every time you catch yourself deceiving yourself. You will begin to see patterns and vulnerabilities. Use this exercise to expand your ability to notice your self-deception.

EXERCISE 2D – SELF-DECEPTION, HANGING ON

Exercise 2 invites you to watch carefully how others think and behave. It is much easier to maintain your self-deception when you stay by yourself. It is only when you notice that others think and act differently than do you, that you more easily see how you might be fooling yourself. When you listen to others speak, see if you hear them talking about life as if it is too hard for them, or if they talk about themselves as if they have no talent. You can make this exercise even more effective if you listen most carefully to people who clearly have their act together more than you. It is not an accident that they have their lives together. They know things that you don't know. It is also likely they don't suffer from the same level of self-deception as do you. The more clearly you see the difference between their way of thinking and yours, the more easily you can modify your point of view.

TASK: Add to your diary insights you gain from noticing the people in your life who have a more effective life than do you.

EXERCISE 3D – SELF-DECEPTION, HANGING ON

Exercise 3 invites you to practice replacing your distortion with a more accurate view of the world. Again, this isn't easy because we all grow accustomed to how we see things. But, when you know your life isn't working, you may be motivated to try something new. All that is required is to take one of the distortions you wrote down in your diary and to replace it with a statement that opens you to new opportunities and greater success.

TASK: Just pick one. If you picked, "I am entitled," substitute, "It is up to me to create what I want." Just write it in your diary and read it every day. Notice how strange it sounds to read it and how resistant you are to acting as if it is true. Notice if you have any resistance to it because you want to cling to your distortion. That is okay. Just read it over three or four times each day until it feels acceptable.

EXERCISE 4D – SELF-DECEPTION, HANGING ON

Exercise 4 invites you to notice that simply reading your new statement over and over begins to create a more positive change. You might first notice a change in your attitude. You started out very resistant to the idea that you could create whatever you want, but you feel the resistance fading. That is a good sign. You might next notice that you feel some excitement about the idea, as if you are looking at things in a way that holds some real possibilities for you. You might even think of something you want to create for yourself and some things you can do to begin making that happen.

TASK: Be easy on yourself. Go slow. Practice with these concepts. Change requires consistent small steps in a new direction.

FACTOR – SELF-DECEPTION

Only if we possess the ability to be honest with ourselves can we cultivate our true purpose.

SELF-ASSESSED RATING - ERODING

You tend to fool yourself about significant issues that make it very difficult to solve your immediate problems.

SESSION 1

EXERCISE 1A – SELF-DECEPTION, ERODING

One of the reasons your life is eroding is because you have too much self-deception to sustain a successful life. This is a difficult topic because it is so difficult to see your self-deception, and yet until you do so, it will continue to keep you from relating to life in a more effective manner. Session 1 focuses your attention on four ways you can be deceiving yourself. Let's get started.

Exercise 1 invites you to see that you might be seeing things that are not there. No, we are not suggesting that you are crazy. But, everyone projects inner thoughts on the world around them. Consider a time when you were in a public place, and the thought came to you that someone looked shady or suspicious. As soon as you entertained that thought, you probably were cautious around them. You may have checked on your wallet or made certain your children were close. The only threat was the one you created in your mind. Could you be creating threats and problems in the world around you that are not there, simply because they are in your mind? Such self-deception becomes reality unless you understand that you saw something that didn't actually exist.

TASK: Over the next week, keep records of the times you catch yourself seeing things that might not be there.

EXERCISE 2A – SELF-DECEPTION, ERODING

Exercise 2 invites you to see that you might have blind spots that keep you from seeing things that actually are real and need to be addressed. Your thoughts may sometimes soothe you and rock you to sleep when you should be alert and vigilant. Perhaps you want to believe that you are well prepared for your job interview because you know the interviewer personally, but get completely blindsided when you are asked questions about your qualifications for which you never prepared. You just thought everything would be okay. You liked that idea, and it let you off the hook for having to put out some effort to get ready. Blind spots have a way of calling you up short in that way. You don't see the hole until you suddenly step in it because you weren't looking for it. You deceived yourself into thinking everything would be fine when there was something to be done.

TASK: See if you can make a list of five times in your life when your blind spots got in the way of your success.

EXERCISE 3A – SELF-DECEPTION, ERODING

Exercise 3 invites you to see that you might have certain biases that act like filters and so distort what you see. It isn't as if you have blind spots. You see everything there is to see, but you have a way of seeing things that isn't exactly the way things are. You might have a bias that you are liked when you are not. Or, that things are stacked against you when they aren't. Or, that you deserve to succeed when you do not. Biases are dangerous because they make it almost impossible to align your efforts with the opportunities at hand. They throw you off. You don't need to be thrown off much to have problems. A ship off course by just a few degrees can end up in a very different place than was intended.

TASK: Make a list of at least five biases that have caused problems in your life.

EXERCISE 4A – SELF-DECEPTION, ERODING

Exercise 4 invites you to see that you can deceive yourself with wishful thinking. This is another distortion that can get you into trouble. Perhaps you are introduced to someone who has an investment opportunity where you can make a killing. It sounds like a once in a lifetime opportunity, and you are so eager to make the money that you don't fully check things out. It is only later when you realized you lost your whole retirement account. You might have wishful thinking about your children's choices, or your health, or any manner of other things. Wishful thinking entices you to not do your homework because you have a good feeling that everything will work out...until it doesn't. Perhaps you fall victim to this self-deception because you easily trust people and have been hurt repeatedly.

TASK: List five times your wishful thinking didn't work out.

SESSION 2

EXERCISE 1B – SELF-DECEPTION, ERODING

Session 2 focuses your attention on the various areas where such self-deception is likely to occur. Let's get started.

Exercise 1 invites you to see that your self-deception can focus on how you view yourself. Not seeing yourself accurately is a serious mistake. There are so many ways to deceive yourself about who you really are. You can see yourself as more or less valuable than you are. You can see yourself as more or less talented than you are. You can see yourself as more or less privileged than you are. The list goes on and on, but every distortion you hold about yourself makes it difficult for you to fit into the life you could have. If you view yourself as more important than you are, you will have unrealistic expectations for your life that can't be sustained. If you view yourself as less important than you are, you will never reach for the accomplishments you could have.

TASK: Write down how you might be deceiving yourself about who you are.

EXERCISE 2B – SELF-DECEPTION, ERODING

Exercise 2 invites you to focus on how you might be deceiving yourself about the people in your life. Again, the possible distortions are almost endless. You can see people as threats, competitors, caretakers, oppressors, dependents, and in a host of other roles. Whenever your view of others is distorted, it seriously throws off your ability to effectively relate. If you see people as threats, you will spend much of your time either on attack or protecting yourself, even when no one is actually threatening you. This will certainly seem odd to others, but may be so detrimental that no one is able or willing to partner with you in any way.

TASK: Make a list of some of the distortions you might have toward the people in your life.

EXERCISE 3B – SELF-DECEPTION, ERODING

Exercise 3 invites you to see how you might be exaggerating the threat to your life. Many people live their lives from the posture of defensiveness. They view almost every interaction as a threat to their wellbeing, either physically or emotionally. They aren't trusting. They aren't open to learn from others. They come from the place of believing they are right about whatever they think, feel, and want. This self-deception insulates you from growing and changing. Rather than learning from whatever is occurring, you wall yourself off, and insist you are right and that whatever is confronting you must be wrong. Cutting yourself off from new points of view almost ensures you will not grow and evolve into a better version of yourself.

TASK: List five ways you might show up being defensive and insisting you are right.

EXERCISE 4B – SELF-DECEPTION, ERODING

Exercise 4 invites you to see how you might miss opportunities. Opportunities are only valuable if you see them as such. If you view them as challenges or as threats, you will not see them for what they are. This self-deception is an entrenchment in how you are in the present moment. Any challenges to your current state, or chances to move beyond your present way of being are seen as negative and detrimental. Your boss might invite you to apply for a new job. You see it as a setup; a chance for him to fire you, and so you pass. But, it wasn't a setup at all. He saw something in you that you don't see in yourself, and wanted to see that potential shine. Because you didn't see it that way, you dug in and missed the opportunity to grow beyond your current life.

TASK: Life five times you missed an opportunity because you deceived yourself into not seeing it as such.

SESSION 3

EXERCISE 1C – SELF-DECEPTION, ERODING

Session 3 focuses your attention on the consequences of your self-deception. Clearly, it is undermining your ability to have a stable and secure life. Let's get started.

Exercise 1 invites you to see that you waste a great deal of energy on foolish pursuits. Your distortion tempts you to invest your energy in fighting battles that would not be battles if you didn't create them. It entices you to be defensive toward people who want to help you. You spend a lot of time and energy justifying your position, even when you position isn't good for you and doesn't get you where you want to go. Wasted energy is a sign of self-deception.

TASK: See if you can list five times you have wasted energy because of ways you have deceived yourself about life.

EXERCISE 2C – SELF-DECEPTION, ERODING

Exercise 2 invites you to notice how your self-deception has led you to be passive even when it would have been more helpful to be active. You have been accepting of things you should have resisted. You have allowed things to occur that you should have fought. You had the opportunity to create new things for your life that you didn't notice, and so remained passive. You didn't think it worth your while to advocate for yourself, and so missed the boat. Passivity rarely is helpful in life. To the extent your self-deception invites you to be passive, it undermines exerting effective control.

TASK: See if you can list five times when you were passive and accepting when it was not in your best interest to do so.

EXERCISE 3C – SELF-DECEPTION, ERODING

Exercise 3 invites you to notice that your self-deception undermines your ability to be aligned with life. Life is happening around you every moment and every day. If you can see what is occurring accurately, you can align with it. When you do, life becomes easy and you move forward without expending a great deal of effort. But, when your self-deception blinds you to see what is naturally unfolding, you are forced to try to create things that aren't naturally happening, or to oppose what is occurring. You are out of step with life, and so destined to a hard road.

TASK: See if you can list five times when you misread the signals and so didn't align properly with life.

EXERCISE 4C – SELF-DECEPTION, ERODING

Exercise 4 invites you to notice that your self-deception results in missing opportunities you did not see. Life provides opportunities almost every day. Every meeting and conversation is pregnant with opportunity when you are open to see and hear without distortion. But, when you come to life with preconceived opinions and judgments, it can be difficult, if not impossible, to recognize them. You may see yourself as a very open person when, in fact, you spend much of your time grinding the same stumps; complaining about your boss, worrying about the future, waiting for someone to rescue you. You are the opposite of open. Your agenda dominates almost everything you do and leaves little room for something new to occur.

TASK: See if you can list five opportunities you missed because you were closed even when you thought you were open.

SESSION 4

EXERCISE 1D – SELF-DECEPTION, ERODING

Session 4 focuses your attention on some changes you can make that will loosen the grip of your self-deception and allow you to better align with life. This isn't easy, because self-deception is difficult to recognize. Let's get started.

Exercise 1 invites you to be constantly on the lookout for ways you are deceiving yourself. It is only when you see it that you can change it. There are some telltale signs, however.

TASK: Notice when you are surprised. When either something good or bad happens that you did not expect, you may have been caught off guard because you had some self-deception that blinded you to what was occurring. Notice when your efforts aren't being rewarded. This too, can be a sign that you are missing something that you need to see. Keep a diary of insights into your self-deception. The better you get at spotting it, the quicker you can escape it.

EXERCISE 2D – SELF-DECEPTION, ERODING

Exercise 2 invites you to notice where you aren't deceiving yourself. There are some aspects of your life that are working well. It is important to recognize them because they help you understand how life works when you are seeing clearly. We want this to be your experience in every part of your life. Perhaps your career is messy but your home life is strong, clear, and solid. You can guess that you have little distortion in your home relationships. Or, you might have lifelong friendships that are mutual and stable, suggesting you see clearly when making and keeping friendships.

TASK: Add these insights to your diary, so you begin to distinguish between those places where you are seeing clearly and where you have self-imposed distortions.

EXERCISE 3D – SELF-DECEPTION, ERODING

Exercise 3 invites you to copy the lives of others. In those areas where your life is messy and you aren't seeing clearly, start paying attention to how more successful people see and act. You may know someone at work whose career is moving along steadily. Get to know this person and listen for how they think about work. Compare it to how you think about it, and see if you have distortions that are making your success difficult. We can all learn from each other. Where one person sees clearly, another doesn't.

TASK: Write your insights in your diary.

EXERCISE 4D – SELF-DECEPTION, ERODING

Exercise 4 invites you to practice being different in areas where you might be deceiving yourself. You wrote down insights from people you know who see things more clearly than do you. Now, you must be willing to use those insights. The difficulty here is often the willingness to change. People may notice and wonder what happened to you. But, unless you change your life will continue to erode. Don't worry about what others think or say. Cherish your life, and make it as strong as you can. If your friend had a positive attitude toward work, while you were always negative and critical, start practicing having a positive attitude. This isn't as difficult as you think. Simply change your mind. Practice being positive and see if things begin to work better. If so, you have escaped one area where you have been deceiving yourself and paying a hefty price.

TASK: Write down one change you will make this week.

FACTOR – SELF-DECEPTION

Only if we possess the ability to be honest with ourselves can we cultivate our true purpose.

SELF-ASSESSED RATING - TREADING WATER

You tend to fool yourself about your giftedness, and the possibilities of cultivating your greatness and a thriving life.

SESSION 1

EXERCISE 1A – SELF-DECEPTION, TREADING WATER

You are treading water because, at least to some extent, you are deceiving yourself too much to be growing. Self-deception makes it difficult for you to read the world around you with sufficient accuracy to move beyond your current level of functioning. Until you understand how you may be deceiving yourself and how you can get past it, you will likely be stuck where you are. Session 1 focuses your attention on some of the ways people tend to deceive themselves. Let's get started.

Exercise 1 invites you to consider the self-deception that you aren't very important. There are certainly many ways in which you are ordinary and like everyone else. But, if you fail to see what is unique about you, you are deceiving yourself. This distortion can let you off the hook with regard to exercising your uniqueness. It allows you to play small. It also keeps your life from being nearly as impactful as it could, and should, be. It is one thing to be humble. It is another thing to be in denial about what you have to offer the world.

TASK: See if you can list five ways you deceive yourself by claiming to be ordinary.

EXERCISE 2A – SELF-DECEPTION, TREADING WATER

Exercise 2 invites you to consider the self-deception of thinking you are more important than, in fact, you are. This is the very opposite of the self-deception considered in Exercise 1. Here, you overestimate your value, and carry yourself as if others should clearly recognize your value and treat you as someone who is very special. You expect certain privileges. You demand special treatment. And, while this might work on occasion, most of the time you are met with resistance and rejection because you have distorted your true value. When you deceive yourself in this manner, you actually invite rejection. You will consistently get feedback that you are over-reaching. If you are wise, you will learn from that feedback and ratchet back your sense of self-importance. If you are in the grip of your self-deception, you will ignore the feedback and persist in carrying yourself in a way you don't deserve. Often, the consequences of doing so only increase as you ignore the warning signs.

TASK: See if you can list five signs that you inflate your importance.

EXERCISE 3A – SELF-DECEPTION, TREADING WATER

Exercise 3 invites you to consider the self-deception of thinking you have insufficient talent to rise beyond your current circumstance. You might be proud of the success you have gained but feel that you have topped out and reached as high a level as you can attain. You keep telling yourself that story, and notice that you aren't given many new opportunities. What you can't see is that your self-deception is broadcasting, to those around you, that you aren't interested in new opportunities. It is more likely to be true that you have reached a level of comfort where you are content, and that you have become a bit lazy. But, rather than admit that to be the truth, you claim you have no more capacity.

TASK: See if you can find at least five signs that you have deceived yourself about your true talent.

EXERCISE 4A – SELF-DECEPTION, TREADING WATER

Exercise 4 invites you to consider the self-deception of thinking you have talents that you don't possess. This can be hugely problematic, as you can get yourself into positions where that talent that you don't possess is required for success. You may think of yourself as a talented musician and because you broadcast yourself as such, someone hires you for an engagement. But, when you show up and play, your audience is alarmed at how poorly you perform. You put yourself in a place of humiliation and rejection because you deceived yourself about the degree of your talent.

TASK: See if you can list five ways you may have exaggerated some talent.

SESSION 2

EXERCISE 1B – SELF-DECEPTION, TREADING WATER

Session 2 focuses your attention on ways your self-deception may be limiting your ability to grow. Let's get started.

Exercise 1 invites you to notice that self-deception makes it very difficult to see where you fit into the world around you. When you don't see yourself or others accurately, it can be almost impossible to understand where you can make a useful contribution. You are likely to put yourself in places where you have little chance of success, and miss those places where success might be predictably secured. For example, if you are deceiving yourself about your wonderful voice, you might continue to face rejection as a singer while missing the value of your talent as a guitarist. What a terrible mistake that would be.

TASK: See if you can make a list of five times when you didn't fit in where you thought you would fit because you were deceiving yourself.

EXERCISE 2B – SELF-DECEPTION, TREADING WATER

Exercise 2 invites you to notice that self-deception makes it very difficult to relate effectively to others. When you are not seeing things the way others see them, much of what you say and do will be "off" in some way. Your perspective will be informed by your idiosyncratic point of view and so out of alignment with what others are saying and thinking. You will come across as odd, at the very least, and perhaps as completely out of touch. It is very difficult to grow as a person when you can't build good alliances with those around you.

TASK: See if you can list at least five times when you could see you weren't relating to others effectively because you were deceiving yourself about something.

EXERCISE 3B – SELF-DECEPTION, TREADING WATER

Exercise 3 invites you to notice that self-deception leads to missteps and mistakes. Because your self-deception about yourself or your life distorts your judgment, you are likely to make less than optimal decisions. Your bias to think you are important leads you to repeatedly insert yourself in places where you aren't welcome. Over and over again, you experience rejection. That rejection bothers you, and causes you to feel resentful and angry. Your anger only makes things worse. Instead of building a track record of successful decisions, your self-deception sets you up to make a series of mistakes. You simply must see clearly and accurately if you are going to be more successful.

TASK: See if you can list five mistakes you have made because you have deceived yourself in some way.

EXERCISE 4B – SELF-DECEPTION, TREADING WATER

Exercise 4 invites you to notice how your self-deception undermines your self-esteem. Often self-deception is constructed to boost self-esteem by seeing yourself in an overly positive light. But, because it isn't real and is contrived in your mind, it doesn't actually work. Thinking you are important and valuable doesn't make you so. When your self-deception faces the light of day, it is exposed and you must then face the fact that you thought wrongly about yourself. Instead of having concentrated on things that would have made you more valuable, you simply acted like you were. This strategy undermines your ability to grow. It is only when you see yourself correctly that your self-esteem will be built on a solid foundation; one that can sustain growth.

TASK: See if you can make a list of five times when your self-esteem has been wounded because you fooled yourself into thinking you were more important than you actually were.

SESSION 3

EXERCISE 1C – SELF-DECEPTION, TREADING WATER

Session 3 focuses your attention on some first steps you can take to begin to move from self-deception into sufficient clarity to begin growing. Let's get started.

Exercise 1 invites you to simply notice what is and isn't working in your life. This is a skill that is fundamental to ending self-deception. The things that work, and keep working well, do so because you are seeing things clearly. It is not an accident that you are experiencing success. It is because you are aligned with life. Those that aren't working, especially where you see a pattern of failure, are good places to begin seeking self-deception. It is highly likely that in these areas, you are fooling yourself about something.

TASK: Make two lists. On one, list all of the areas of your life that work well and have been working well. On the second list, write down all of the areas of your life where you aren't experiencing consistent success. Look at these areas and write down what you might be missing or distorting that is causing failure.

EXERCISE 2C – SELF-DECEPTION, TREADING WATER

Exercise 2 invites you to invite feedback. The input of others can be extremely helpful in identifying those areas of our lives where we are deceiving ourselves. Everyone has his or her own distortions but, if you ask enough people the same question, you can begin to discern what is really going on. Get used to asking people how you might be deceiving yourself. Write down whatever they tell you. Rather than telling them why they are wrong, practice looking for what might be true in their feedback. They might not be completely accurate, but there still might be important things for you to learn in what they tell you.

TASK: Practice asking people you trust to tell you their truth for feedback, rather than selecting only those who will say what they think you want to hear. Make a list of five people you imagine would give you the most honest feedback. Ask each one this week where you might be deceiving yourself. Write down whatever they tell you.

EXERCISE 3C – SELF-DECEPTION, TREADING WATER

Exercise 3 invites you to take defensiveness as a sign there is something you might need to face that you are avoiding. When you get defensive about feedback, almost always it is because you know there is truth in it. It is almost as if your defensiveness is trying to get you out of facing reality by making it painful for the person confronting you. Imagine that you asked for feedback and were told you are lazy. You don't like to think of yourself that way, so you get angry at the person who said you were lazy. But, they said it for a reason. You do something that seems lazy to them. If you can come to see how you are lazy and how it is holding you back, you have an opportunity to change. Their feedback is a wonderful gift.

TASK: Begin to notice when you become defensive. As soon as you see yourself reacting that way, ask what reality you might be avoiding. Practice doing this every day for the next week.

EXERCISE 4C – SELF-DECEPTION, TREADING WATER

Exercise 4 invites you to accept what is so about yourself. This might sound a bit strange, but it is so important that you come to see and accept the truth, and the whole truth, about your life. You might not be as successful as you would like to be, but accepting whatever success you have is the beginning of creating more success. On the other hand, pretending you are as successful as you want to be when, in fact, you are not only sets you up for greater failure. Acceptance of yourself is fundamental to giving up self-deception. Practice accepting yourself as perfect just as you are. That doesn't mean you can't get better. But, it does mean that your uniqueness is your greatest asset. The more you accept yourself, the more your uniqueness can shine.

TASK: Make a list of areas where you aren't accepting yourself just as you are, and practice extending acceptance to yourself every day.

SESSION 4

EXERCISE 1D – SELF-DECEPTION, TREADING WATER

Session 4 focuses your attention on building on the insights you gained from the last session. Let's get started.

Exercise 1 invites you to build on what is working in your life. You noticed that you do some things well, and do so consistently. In those areas you almost always get good results and positive feedback. Perhaps people tell you that you are a great mother, or a wonderful friend. It doesn't matter how big or small is your area of consistent success. What does matter, is that you embrace it and identify what it is that is special about you in this area of your life. Perhaps you have a compassionate heart, or you are extremely loyal. Whatever is the key to your success is the thing you should expand. If your compassion makes you successful, practice being more compassionate. If your hard work makes you successful, practice working harder. Your growth will come from being your natural self in areas where you are gifted.

TASK: Write down what makes you successful in the areas of your life where you experience consistent success. List five ways you can expand on this gift.

EXERCISE 2D – SELF-DECEPTION, TREADING WATER

Exercise 2 invites you to accept the fact that in other areas of your life, you aren't gifted. It doesn't matter nearly as much who you want to be, as it does that you be the person you are. No one is good at everything. Accepting your weakness is key to giving up self-deception. Don't pretend to be gifted where you are not. Don't pretend to be more successful than you are. Don't pretend to be strong where you are weak. It is okay to have weaknesses. Embrace them, and learn to avoid those areas of life that require strength where you are weak. You might be a very compassionate person, but not very courageous. Don't pretend to be courageous. Leave that up to someone else. Just focus on being compassionate. Your weaknesses are meant to guide you every bit as much as are your strengths.

TASK: List your greatest weaknesses and what they teach you to avoid.

EXERCISE 3D – SELF-DECEPTION, TREADING WATER

Exercise 3 invites you to progress slowly, one step at a time. Sometimes self-deception is fueled by the desire to create success too quickly. Rather than building on a solid foundation, it is an effort to jump to the head of the line by pretending to be who you are not, or that you are better than you actually are. You want to be considered the lead sales person at your company, and so you pretend you have more leads than you have. People respect you for your talk, but inwardly you are anxious because you know you have to actually bring in the sales by the end of the year. When you don't, you get fired. It would have been far better if you had set lower expectations for yourself and allowed them to grow as you gained experience. Your impatience set you up for failure. Growing slowly and steadily is far more sustainable.

TASK: When you consider where you want to grow, list five baby steps you can take to move in that direction. Commit to putting those to work in your life.

EXERCISE 4D – SELF-DECEPTION, TREADING WATER

Exercise 4 invites you to keep being true to yourself. As you uncover your self-deception, you have the opportunity to make changes that reveal more of your true self. This is an endless process of self-discovery. The more you learn who you are, the better you know who you are not and who you truly are. Every lesson then provides the opportunity to change how you show up in your world. Snakes grow by shedding their skin. Crabs grow by moving out of their old shell for a bigger one. They let go of who they were to become a bigger version of themselves. It is important that you get comfortable with showing up differently with the people in your life and in your life circumstances.

TASK: Make a list of some the ways you need to show your uniqueness more clearly to the world, and how you will do so.

FACTOR – SELF-DECEPTION

Only if we possess the ability to be honest with ourselves, can we cultivate our true purpose.

SELF-ASSESSED RATING - GROWING

You tend to see the world fairly accurately, except in one or two areas of insecurity or weakness.

SESSION 1

EXERCISE 1A – SELF-DECEPTION, GROWING

You are growing, at least partly, because you don't often deceive yourself about who you are and the nature of the world around you. Yet, you are not thriving. Perhaps there are some places where you aren't fully aware or willing to be aware of things for which you need to take responsibility. These exercises are designed to hunt for those issues and to bring them to your attention, as well as to guide you past them. Session 1 focuses your attention on places where you might be suffering from self-deception. Let's get started.

Exercise 1 invites you to consider times when you either consciously or unconsciously exaggerate your success in some way. You might find yourself boasting about something that went well for you in the past, or getting a good feeling from looking younger than many of your friends. Exaggerations of this sort suggest some hidden insecurity or sense of inadequacy; some part of yourself that you don't like or fully accept.

TASK: Just be on the lookout for times you do this over the next week, and take the time to wonder why you are exaggerating. Why are you trying to deceive others and yourself as to your competence and capability?

EXERCISE 2A – SELF-DECEPTION, GROWING

Exercise 2 invites you to notice if you deceive yourself by being unwilling to acknowledge all of your gifts. Sometimes it is our greatness that we are most fearful of seeing and accepting, because with our greatness comes some responsibility that can be burdensome and scary. You may not want to know that you have a wonderful gift of compassion, because somewhere inside you understand that if you get in touch with it, you will need to find some way of caring for the homeless or feed hungry children. You have a good life. Things are going well. Why complicate your life in some way that most other people don't and won't. But, thriving is a level of living not many reach. It requires being honest and open about all of who you are.

TASK: See if you can get in touch with the idea that you might be fooling yourself and others that there is nothing all that special about you. Just answer this question honestly, "Are you holding back on parts of who you really are?"

EXERCISE 3A – SELF-DECEPTION, GROWING

Exercise 3 invites you to notice if you are deceiving yourself about a problem in your life. It is obvious that you are doing well in so many ways. Because your life is good, it may be easy for you to overlook one or two minor problems. They aren't really disrupting anything, but they might be keeping you from thriving. Perhaps you have just a few secrets you are keeping from your spouse. They are about things in the past, so why not just forget about them? But, if you pay attention, you may notice that they introduce a slight bit of guilt and fear to your relationship, which keeps you from being as open and intimate as you used to be. Or, you might have your act together in many ways, but you are 40 pounds overweight. You know you should lose weight, but you ignore it. You fool yourself into thinking that it is okay to have these one or two minor problems.

TASK: Make a list of any problems you are deceiving yourself about.

EXERCISE 4A – SELF-DECEPTION, GROWING

Exercise 4 invites you to notice if you are deceiving yourself about some weakness you have. You like your strengths and gifts. You talk about them all of the time. But, you hardly ever, or never, talk about your weaknesses. It is almost as if you aren't allowed to have any. You are probably fairly accepting of the weaknesses in others and you will readily say that everyone has them, but you don't like to think you have any. You dont like to own your weaknesses because they make you feel vulnerable and needy. This self-deception gets in the way of a deeper connection with the people in your life, because it limits your humility and blocks your ability to openly share all of yourself.

TASK: See if you can list five times when you have avoided owning and admitting some weakness.

SESSION 2

EXERCISE 1B – SELF-DECEPTION, GROWING

Session 2 invites you to focus on places you can look to stop self-deception. While it is not easy to see, self-deception creates problems that leave important clues. Let's get started.

Exercise 1 invites you to look at any areas where your life isn't working well and to wonder if the cause of the problem is something about which you are deceiving yourself. You are growing because you see things and yourself fairly clearly and accurately. This allows you to understand what is going on and how to join in successfully. Areas of your life that aren't working are good places to assume you aren't seeing something correctly because you are fooling yourself.

TASK: Make a list of any situations that aren't working as they should. Next to each, make a list of hunches you have about ways you might be deceiving yourself.

EXERCISE 2B – SELF-DECEPTION, GROWING

Exercise 2 invites you to look at things that frustrate you for signs you might be deceiving yourself. Frustration often occurs when things don't go as we imagined they would, or when we have expectations that are not met. Consider some of the frustrations you experience in your daily life. Perhaps you get frustrated by the way other people drive. Or, you might get frustrated with your children when they don't behave. Ask yourself what you might be missing that, if you saw it, would remove that frustration. It is here you might productively seek to understand how you are deceiving yourself.

TASK: Make a list of your most common frustrations. Next to each, write down any guesses you have about your self-deception.

EXERCISE 3B – SELF-DECEPTION, GROWING

Exercise 3 invites you to notice where you get stuck. Your career may have progressed well until you got to a certain level, and then it screeched to a halt. Or, your marriage might have been getting closer and more satisfying, until it began to idle. It isn't that anything is wrong, but you can't seem to see the next step that would get things moving along. That inability to clearly see the next step can be a symptom of self-deception. You can't see what needs to be seen because you are committed to either seeing something that is not there, or not seeing something that is. Perhaps you don't yet possess that one skill you need for your career to advance, but you have been telling yourself that it isn't that important. Or, perhaps you have been telling yourself that your spouse is wildly in love with you even though she hasn't been saying that to you lately.

TASK: Make a list of places where you are stuck. Write down your guesses about what you might not be seeing or what you might be seeing that isn't real.

EXERCISE 4B – SELF-DECEPTION, GROWING

Exercise 4 invites you to notice where you are having conflict. Conflict is a kind of friction that often occurs because one or both parties is deceiving him or herself. Your friend is angry and telling you that you are insensitive. You are angry and arguing back that you certainly are not insensitive. Instead, they are insensitive. You are clearly in conflict. You feel accused and are fighting back. You don't even realize that you are proving the point that you are insensitive in the way you are reacting. You are fooling yourself that you are always a very sensitive person. You like that view of yourself and don't want to admit that, at times, you can be self-centered and insensitive. Conflict shines a bright light on our self-deception.

TASK: See if you can write down five times when you were having a conflict, and the self-deception that fueled it.

SESSION 3

EXERCISE 1C – SELF-DECEPTION, GROWING

Session 3 focuses your attention of commitments you can take that begin to open your eyes to your self-deception. Let's get started.

Exercise 1 invites you to the commitment of being honest with yourself. Being honest with yourself means that you place honesty over trying to look good, protecting yourself, covering your mistakes, and every other way you pretend in order to get by. Being honest means that you are willing to accept yourself as you are, privately and publically. You are comfortable asking for help, admitting when you don't know something, owning your mistakes, and expressing your needs and weaknesses. Being honest means seeing clearly where you are gifted and where you are not. It is a big commitment.

TASK: See if you are willing to make this commitment to yourself. Try saying it out loud. "I am fundamentally committed to being honest with myself." Notice if you hesitate when you say it or have reluctance. Practice saying it until you own it.

EXERCISE 2C – SELF-DECEPTION, GROWING

Exercise 2 invites you to the commitment of facing problems squarely. You may catch yourself saying you already do this. And, you are probably right...most of the time. But, we are asking you to face every problem all of the time. You might overlook a problem because you fear addressing it would create its own problem. For example, your spouse drinks too much, but you won't tell him because he is sensitive about it. Or, you disagree with your boss, but you won't tell her because you might get into trouble. Avoiding problems means they don't go away and often they only get worse. Thriving requires a clear path ahead. You can't get there when you have hidden land mines of unresolved problems.

TASK: Make a list of all of your unresolved problems, and see if you will commit to resolving all of them.

EXERCISE 3C – SELF-DECEPTION, GROWING

Exercise 3 invites you to the commitment of resolving conflicts directly. It is easy to choose to disagree in order to keep the peace. It is easy to walk away from a conflict while holding onto some secret anger, resentment, or frustration. You put on a happy face and it looks like everything is okay, but it isn't and you know it. You are being deceptive. If you live with conflicts such as these long enough, you will grow accustomed to how you feel about the person and might even think everything is okay between the two of you. But, you are deceiving yourself. Unresolved conflicts are like cancer. They slowly grow until they kill the relationship. If you are going to thrive, you must be committed to resolving all conflicts so you are harboring no bad feelings.

TASK: Are you willing to commit to this? If so, write it down.

EXERCISE 4C – SELF-DECEPTION, GROWING

Exercise 4 invites you to the commitment of accepting uncertainty. Perhaps the fundamental reason we deceive others and ourselves is to try to avoid the uncertainty of life. We think we know how we want things to turn out and what needs to happen in order to make that happen. We then become who we need to be to make that happen. If we want friends, we pretend to be friendly. If we want to succeed at work, we pretend to agree with the boss. If we want our partner to be happy, we keep secrets and lie. We fool ourselves into thinking we are people we are not in order to try to control outcomes. This is a huge mistake. It is only when you commit to accepting uncertainty that you will be free to be yourself and to give up your self-deception. You don't know how things will turn out, but you do know you will be yourself. You will speak your truth. You will state your preferences. You will share what you know. This is a radical commitment.

TASK: Write it down and then read it out loud. See if you are willing to commit to it.

SESSION 4

EXERCISE 1D – SELF-DECEPTION, GROWING

Session 4 recommends some things you can do that will lessen your self-deception and will foster a life of thriving. Let's get started.

Exercise 1 invites you to face what is most important in every moment. Every moment of every day presents an opportunity. Many people miss them because they distract themselves with things, thoughts, words, and actions that fill up space but don't move the needle very much, if at all. Begin listening to people talk. Notice how much of what they say is unimportant. You might be asked how you are doing and you answer "fine." That means nothing. You might talk about the weather, or your favorite sports team, or some gossip. Despite having talked for quite some time, nothing of importance occurred. Nothing new was learned. Nothing changes as a result of the conversation. Yet, if both people were listening for and willing to address the opportunity, that same conversation may have had the ability to radically transform both lives.

TASK: Practice today listening for what is most important in every moment.

EXERCISE 2D – SELF-DECEPTION, GROWING

Exercise 2 invites you to begin having fierce conversations with yourself. That term refers to a book by that title, written by Susan Scott. The idea is to learn how to interrogate yourself about the most important thing that you need to do, face, or decide in every moment. To be good at having fierce conversations with yourself, you must notice when you are being fearful or timid and beginning to turn away from an issue. It is here that you begin your interrogation. Ask yourself what you are afraid of. Then, ask what will happen if you avoid what you don't want to face. Next, ask what you would do if you faced it directly. Next, ask what you might gain if you dealt with it.

TASK: Practice having fierce conversations every day in order to move into places where you might be tempted to deceive yourself.

EXERCISE 3D – SELF-DECEPTION, GROWING

Exercise 3 invites you to begin having fierce conversations with others. Just as you practiced using fierce conversations to step into issues that need to be faced, you will benefit greatly from having such conversations with the important people in your life. Relationships can easily accumulate issues that are avoided rather than addressed. Slights, misunderstandings, mistakes, and disloyalty can be avoided for the sake of superficial harmony. But, the result is less functionality and intimacy. It is only by having fierce conversations that you clean out any issues that might undermine your relationships, and build the kind of interaction that will support each other being the best version of yourselves every day. Use the same questions from Exercise 2 with the people in your life.

TASK: Pick one person whom you care about and engage in a fierce conversation today. See if you don't experience more aliveness as a result.

EXERCISE 4D – SELF-DECEPTION, GROWING

Exercise 4 invites you to practice being courageous. Being courageous doesn't mean that you don't get scared. It does mean that when you are scared, you move forward rather than retreating. It is only by being courageous that you will keep finding and removing any self-deception that remains. We sometimes ask the people we coach if they are good people. Everyone says yes. We then ask if they are bad people. No one wants to think of themselves as bad. When asked if they have done bad things, everyone says they have but are quite reluctant to share what bad deeds they have done. They want to deceive themselves about their goodness. They don't want to accept that they are both good and bad all at the same time and can choose either in each moment. It takes courage to step into such clear and powerful awareness.

TASK: Practice courage each day by noticing when you are afraid of something, and then moving toward it.

EXERCISE SERIES: SPIRITUALITY

FACTOR – SPIRITUALITY

While we are not preaching any theology, we are advocating that spirituality is a necessary component to finding your true purpose. Spirituality simply acknowledges that the Universe is bigger than you.

SELF-ASSESSED RATING - HANGING ON

You fail to see or comprehend anything beyond the immediate and material, and so don't benefit from the influence of spirituality to hardly any extent.

SESSION 1

EXERCISE 1A – SPIRITUALITY, HANGING ON

You are hanging on by your fingernails, at least partly, due to the fact that you have no awareness of life beyond that which is material. The purpose of these exercises is to make your lack of spirituality more visible to you, and to point out some of the ways it is severely limiting your life. More awareness is the first step of change. Having no understanding of spirituality is like looking at life through a very small tube. What you see is real, but it is only a very small portion of all there is to see. If you take what you see to be the whole, you are destined to have a distorted and limited view of the world around you. Session 1 focuses your attention on a variety of ways a lack of spirituality shows up in life. Let's get started.

Exercise 1 invites you to see that the first sign of no spirituality is a total focus on material things. Life is only about what you own for you. The quality and design of your clothes matters to you. The size and condition of your house matters to you. The price of the car you drive matters. In fact, those kinds of things are the only things that matter. You can't imagine there is anything else that could or should matter to you.

TASK: Take a few moments to notice if this is true about you. Rate yourself from 1 (totally true) to 5 (not true at all).

EXERCISE 2A – SPIRITUALITY, HANGING ON

Exercise 2 invites you to see that the second sign of no spirituality is a total focus on pleasure. Life is only about what feels good to you if you lack awareness of spirituality. You indulge your desires as much as you can. You eat too much food. You drink too much alcohol. You do what feels good as much as and whenever you can. You can't imagine there is any reason to hold back. You can't imagine there is anything more meaningful than your pleasure. Your life is short and you are going to take advantage of every opportunity to feel good.

TASK: Take a few moments to notice if this is true about you. Rate yourself from 1 (totally true) to 5 (not true at all).

EXERCISE 3A – SPIRITUALITY, HANGING ON

Exercise 3 invites you to see that the third sign of no spirituality is self-focus. Your life is all about you. You aren't really interested in the welfare of anyone but yourself. You might pretend to care, but probably not. You see your task in life is making yourself as comfortable and happy as you can be, and you don't care much about the consequences of your pursuit and how it might impact others. You like to talk about yourself. You think about yourself. You only do what is in your best interest.

TASK: Take a few moments to notice if this is true about you. Rate yourself from 1 (totally true) to 5 (not true at all).

EXERCISE 4A – SPIRITUALITY, HANGING ON

Exercise 4 invites you to see that the fourth sign of no spirituality is an excessive focus on the present and near term. You don't concern yourself with things like the ecology of the world or the welfare of the poor, because those are long term problems. You won't be around all that long, so those aren't things you either care about or think about. You are focused on how to make your life as good as it can be today and for the few short years you are alive. You are motivated to make as much money as you can while expending the least amount of effort as possible, in the hope that you can quickly make enough to quit and indulge yourself for the rest of your life. Your dreams are about the places you will see, the restaurants you will eat in, and the comfort and security you will have. Your view is to take advantage as best you can of the opportunity before you to create as pleasurable and comfortable a life as is possible. There is no more.

TASK: Take a few moments to notice if this is true about you. Rate yourself from 1 (totally true) to 5 (not true at all).

SESSION 2

EXERCISE 1B – SPIRITUALITY, HANGING ON

Session 2 focuses your attention on some of the limitations the lack of spirituality imposes on your life and contributes to the fact you are hanging on by your fingernails. Let's get started.

Exercise 1 invites you to see that the lack of spirituality limits your ability to wonder. Wonder is a trait that expands your life by feeding your curiosity about what you don't know. Life is filled with mysteries that are beyond our current understanding. Imagine that not that long ago, mankind believed the world was flat and that the Universe revolved around the earth. Modern science continues to discover particles that are the foundation of matter and planets that may have life-sustaining atmosphere. There is so much to know beyond what you know. But wonder is not important if you don't believe there is anything beyond today's pleasure and the limits of the material. Instead of being curious, you remain limited in your knowledge and ignorant. It is wonder that presses discovery.

TASK: Take a few moments to notice if this is true about you. Rate your level of wonder from 1 (It is absent) to 5 (It is quite high).

EXERCISE 2B – SPIRITUALITY, HANGING ON

Exercise 2 invites you to notice that the lack of spirituality limits your capacity to notice experience and share love. Love is not material. It can't be bought or sold, saved or traded. Love moves in the opposite direction from selfishness. It prompts us to sacrifice and even to suffer for the object of our love. The appreciation of love is a spiritual quality. Those who are not in touch with spirituality cannot see the value of love or open themselves to its influence. Whatever richness love brings to a life is absent.

TASK: Take a few moments to consider your capacity for experiencing and sharing love. Rate your life from 1 (very little capacity) to 5 (very high capacity).

EXERCISE 3B – SPIRITUALITY, HANGING ON

Exercise 3 invites you to see that the third sign of a lack of spirituality is self-focus. Your life is all about you. You aren't really interested in the welfare of anyone but yourself and perhaps your very small circle of family and friends. And, perhaps, if you are honest, you might notice that your interest in those you do care about is really a manifestation of self-interest. You don't want anything bad happening to them because of its impact on you. Self-centeredness isn't necessarily the same as selfishness. It simply means that you are the center of your world because you know of nothing more important than yourself.

TASK: Take a few moments to consider the degree of your self-focus. Rate yourself from 1 (very self-focused) to 5 (not self-focused at all).

EXERCISE 4B – SPIRITUALITY, HANGING ON

Exercise 4 invites you to see that the fourth sign of a lack of spirituality is pettiness. Because you don't have a very big perspective on life, small issues seem big and big issues don't show up. You don't think much about issues like meaning and purpose. You don't like to reflect on topics like values. You don't concern yourself with making a contribution to the world around you. Without any interest in such things, you find yourself talking about ordinary things like what sports teams won this week, the new grocery store coming into your neighborhood, and gossip about the neighbors. Perhaps everyone talks about such things from time to time, but you may notice that this is all you have to talk about. It is your life.

TASK: Listen to the things you talk about over the next week. Ask yourself if they tend to be petty. Rate your conversations from 1 (quite petty) to 5 (not petty at all).

SESSION 3

EXERCISE 1C – SPIRITUALITY, HANGING ON

Session 3 focuses your attention on some of the implications of having very limited spirituality for the quality and success of your life. Let's get started.

Exercise 1 invites you to see that when you have no awareness of life beyond the material, you are missing the big picture. You are only seeing a small portion of what there is to see. Hence, everything about your life is likely to be out of kilter with reality. You are living as someone who was born blind and has no experience of a life of sight. For you it is normal to fumble around in the dark with no appreciation of how different life would be if you could see. It is so easy for you to make mistakes in judgment. It is so easy for you to miss the true joy and peace of life. You may not easily identify this as true about your life, and may have an easier time seeing your limitation if you compare your life to that of someone who is functioning at a much higher level.

TASK: Pick two or three people you know whose quality of life is much higher than yours. See if you can identify three ways they demonstrate some understanding of spirituality.

EXERCISE 2C – SPIRITUALITY, HANGING ON

Exercise 2 invites you to notice how easy it is for you to experience life as if it is happening to you. You aren't able to see many patterns in your life. Not only can't you see how you create the problems you experience, but because you fail to access spirituality you don't understand spiritual principles and how they impact life. You don't understand how selflessness invites others to help you. You don't see how caring for the world increases your impact as a human being. Instead, it seems as if life is random and you have no clue as to why it isn't working better for you. You likely complain and feel like a victim but don't know what to do to create order and success.

TASK: Pay attention to how you talk about your life over the next week. List five times when you spoke about life as if it were happening to you.

EXERCISE 3C – SPIRITUALITY, HANGING ON

Exercise 3 invites you to notice how often you act as a victim because you aren't spiritual. When you see your life as out of your control, you act as if there is nothing you can do to manage it. As bad things happen seemingly randomly, all you can do is react to the latest crisis and hold on. Your life spirals downward in disarray. You might notice this happening to you in many areas of your life. Perhaps long ago you thought you had a successful career in front of you, but now you are barely holding onto your job. Or, perhaps you have been married and divorced multiple times and have no idea how to create a successful relationship. Or, perhaps you have been in the grip of some addiction that you tried to break free of, but it still controls your life. Acting like a victim is often the result of the lack of spirituality.

TASK: List five ways you experience life as if you are a victim.

EXERCISE 4C – SPIRITUALITY, HANGING ON

Exercise 4 invites you to see that the quality of your life suffers as a result of the absence of spirituality. Not only aren't things going well for you, but instead of your life becoming richer it is becoming poorer. Successes aren't building on previous successes to create a stable foundation for your life. Relationships aren't becoming deeper and more satisfying. In fact, quite the opposite is true. As the years pass you find yourself more anxious and depressed. Your interests are narrowing. You feel stuck in a rut from which you can't escape. It is almost as if you can feel the goodness of your life slipping from you but don't know what to do about it.

TASK: See if you can list five ways the richness of your life has diminished over the past few years.

SESSION 4

EXERCISE 1D – SPIRITUALITY, HANGING ON

Session 4 focuses your attention on some ways you can begin to cultivate at least the most basic awareness of spirituality. Let's get started.

Exercise 1 invites you to open your eyes to a bigger picture. This is quite easy to do. Go out at night and look at the stars. Or, go to the beach and look at the ocean. See how vast both are; how endless they seem to be. Imagine how many stars are in the Universe and how many planets surround those stars. Can you contemplate something as big as the Universe, or even the ocean, and not feel quite small by comparison? Imagine all there is to know that you don't know. Imagine all of the questions to ask that you don't ever ask. You can explain so little about what you see. It is the vast unknown. Considering the unknown and the unknowable is a path toward spirituality. Such a grand view of life creates a new context for your life. It will begin to rearrange your priorities and open you to new ways of thinking.

TASK: Make time every day for the next month to see the stars and to contemplate, even if only for five minutes, the vastness of things.

EXERCISE 2D – SPIRITUALITY, HANGING ON

Exercise 2 invites you to take time to notice innocence. There is something about babies, all babies, which is amazing. Most people are naturally drawn toward puppies, kittens, and infant children because they radiate an innocence and openness that we find attractive. It isn't because they are especially useful. Their innocence is a reminder of a time when you had that same innocence. You were not yet jaded, soured, and beaten down. You radiated something beautiful. We contend that that innocence is spiritual at its core. The more you notice such innocence and allow it to impact you, the more your eyes will open to the world of spirit. Take time this week to stop in a pet store and to play with the puppies and kittens if you are allowed. Perhaps you know someone with an infant or small child and can pay a visit.

TASK: Pay attention to the innocence and feel your draw toward it.

EXERCISE 3D – SPIRITUALITY, HANGING ON

Exercise 3 invites you to take time to notice beauty. Every morning the sun rises and every evening it sets. When the sky is clear there is often an amazingly beautiful sunrise and sunset. How often to you stop, pull your car to the side of the road, and give yourself to the beauty in the sky? Nature is filled with amazing and remarkable beauty. Take a walk in the woods or along the beach, and take in the beauty that is all around you. Ask yourself, "What is the source of this beauty?" It is abundant and it is free. Both the rich and the poor have equal access to it. It is everywhere and it points to some source that is beautiful beyond our contemplation. Noticing beauty will open your eyes to the world of spirit.

TASK: Find five minutes each day for the next month to notice beauty.

EXERCISE 4D – SPIRITUALITY, HANGING ON

Consider attending a place of worship. Doing so isn't necessary to discover the world of spirit, but it is one possible avenue. Some places of worship focus more fully on the world of spirit than do others, but every religious tradition is filled with spirit at its core. Stories of the lives of spiritual people may inspire you. Sacred literature can open your eyes.

TASK: Look for a place that connects with you in some deep way. If one doesn't, try another until you find one that does. Be willing to try places of worship that are different from your spiritual tradition if you have one.

FACTOR – SPIRITUALITY

While we are not preaching any theology, we are advocating that spirituality is a necessary component to finding your true purpose. Spirituality simply acknowledges that the Universe is bigger than you.

SELF-ASSESSED RATING - ERODING

You have glimpses of spirituality, but fail to understand how to cultivate them or connect them with your life.

SESSION 1

EXERCISE 1A – SPIRITUALITY, ERODING

Your life is eroding, at least partly, because your awareness of spirituality and its role in your life is less than adequate. These exercises are designed to help you better understand spirituality and how you might cultivate this dimension of your life experience. Session 1 focuses your attention on understanding spirituality. First, we want to differentiate it from being religious. While certainly many people who are religious are spiritual, some are not. It is also true that some people who aren't particularly religious are quite spiritual. They are two different things. Let's get started.

Exercise 1 invites you to see that spirituality is awareness that there is something more to life than only the tangible and material. Much in life is material; it can be bought and sold, saved and spent, owned and used. But, not everything in life is like that. Things like love, beauty, inspiration, and goodness are from a different realm of life. None of them can be bought, sold, stored, or spent.

TASK: See if you can make a list of 10 things that belong to the world of spirit.

EXERCISE 2A – SPIRITUALITY, ERODING

Exercise 2 invites you to see that the world of spirit provides context for your life. The questions spirit addresses about life have to do with meaning, purpose, and eternity. They are big questions. It may be impossible to completely answer these questions but simply contemplating them has a profound impact. Asking yourself questions like these causes you to think about your life in a different way. Things that other people think are very important, like the type of car you drive, or where you get your hair done, become far less important in light of such big questions.

TASK: See if you can make a list of five big questions.

EXERCISE 3A – SPIRITUALITY, ERODING

Exercise 3 invites you to see that the world of spirit provides values that enrich life. Values such as love, joy, peace, patience, kindness, gentleness, generosity, and self-control are spiritual values. Notice that none of them is particularly valuable in helping you make more money or buy a bigger house…at least not in an obvious way. But, each one contributes something to the quality of your experience of being alive. They make you a richer person in spirit. And, some might argue that they make you a richer person than those who have great material resources but lack such values. That is for you to decide.

TASK: List as many values as you can think of that fit this definition of spiritual.

EXERCISE 4A – SPIRITUALITY, ERODING

Exercise 4 invites you to see that the world of spirit provides guidance for life. Some choices enhance your spirituality while others detract from it. As you pursue growth in the world of spirit, you learn to make choices that not only make your character richer, they also are the foundation of a materially successful life. For example, a spiritual value is to show respect for others. You might be able to achieve short term gain by ripping people off, but at the price of broken relationships, few allies, and a great deal of resentment toward you. On the other hand, when you come from a place of showing deep respect to everyone, you build win/win relationships that last a lifetime and are filled with goodwill toward you. Your life prospers as the people whom you have shown respect reciprocate.

TASK: See if you can list five ways spirituality might provide useful guidance for your life.

SESSION 2

EXERCISE 1B – SPIRITUALITY, ERODING

Session 2 focuses your attention on signs that your spirituality is not sufficient to support a successful life. Let's get started.

Exercise 1 invites you to see that when you lack sufficient spirituality you tend to be shortsighted. You don't have a very big view of your life. Your biggest questions are things like, "How can I keep my job?", "How can I make a little more money?", or "How can I avoid my partner's anger?" These are all reasonable questions, but they aren't big questions. They don't lead you to see the interconnectedness of things. You end up trying to solve each concern as if it stood by itself. You can't see that there is a different way for you to operate that might solve all of these issues. If there is such a different way, you certainly don't know what it is.

TASK: See if you can list five ways that you have been shortsighted and so have suffered some frustration or loss.

EXERCISE 2B – SPIRITUALITY, ERODING

Exercise 2 invites you to see that when you lack sufficient spirituality you tend to be too self-focused. Your reference point for almost everything is, "How does this affect me?" Again, there is nothing wrong with considering your own needs and wants, but you aren't the center of the Universe. People who concern themselves too much with how things impact them fail to see how those same things impact others. They don't have much ability to truly appreciate the needs, opinions, and thoughts of others. You may know someone who is too self-focused. You are telling them a story about something that happened to you, and before you finish they are telling you about a similar thing that happened to them. They can't seem to let you have your story without making it about them. Could this also be you?

TASK: List five ways you might tend to be overly self-focused.

EXERCISE 3B – SPIRITUALITY, ERODING

Exercise 3 invites you to see that when you lack sufficient spirituality you tend to lack a meaningful sense of purpose. Your purpose seems to be more about survival. You spend much of your time trying to make enough money to give your kids a decent home and education. Then you focus on having enough money in savings for a secure retirement. Your purpose is dominated by fear of falling short and of being at the mercy of life. Spirituality is meant to supply purpose to your life that is filled with a sense of security and peace. It goes way beyond managing the uncertainties of life to a higher plane; one in which you see how your gifts and talents can make a difference in the world.

TASK: See if you can write down the purpose of your life. Does it seem to be big enough or dominated by anxiety?

EXERCISE 4B – SPIRITUALITY, ERODING

Exercise 4 invites you to see that when you lack sufficient spirituality you tend to suffer from excessive worry. Life can seem very difficult when it feels like everything rests on your shoulders, and you feel responsible not only for your own success but also for that of people you love. There is so much you don't control. There is only so much you can do no matter how hard you work and how much you care. You are aware of the possibility of failure and that possibility might haunt you day and night. "What will happen to my family if I lose my job?", or "How will I save enough money to put the kids through school?" The worry can erode your quality of life and become so burdensome that you become resentful of the responsibilities you have assumed.

TASK: See if you can list five circumstances about which you tend to worry a great deal.

SESSION 3

EXERCISE 1C – SPIRITUALITY, ERODING

Session 3 focuses your attention on the results created when you lack sufficient spirituality. Let's get started.

Exercise 1 invites you to see that you tend to define yourself and your life in terms of your possessions and accomplishments. There is certainly nothing wrong with taking pride in your possessions and accomplishments, but if you are making too much of them you are missing the deeper truth that you are much more than both. It is only when you can view yourself through spiritual eyes that you can see the value of your being and not just your doing. Real self-esteem is rooted in this bedrock. Without the ability to see your true value, your sense of self easily vacillates depending on your current circumstance. When things are going well, you feel great about yourself. When things are going poorly, you are filled with anxiety and self-doubt.

TASK: Write down your answer to the question, "Who am I?" Notice if your answer is filled with references to your possessions and accomplishments, or if it is grounded in the deeper truth of who you are.

EXERCISE 2C – SPIRITUALITY, ERODING

Exercise 2 invites you to notice that when you have insufficient spirituality, your life becomes about endless striving. You never seem to have enough. You don't have enough money, enough time, enough love, and enough fun. The list can go on and on. You expend a lot of effort trying to succeed, but it never seems like you get there. In fact, despite your effort it seems as if your life is sliding backward. When you become aware that things are not going well, you might redouble your effort, but it doesn't seem to help. Your striving is using up your energy and resources but not accomplishing much.

TASK: Notice your striving. Are you still committed to trying to work harder to get where you want to be, or have you given up because it is simply too difficult?

EXERCISE 3C – SPIRITUALITY, ERODING

Exercise 3 invites you to notice that when you have insufficient spirituality you feel an emptiness that is difficult to fill. Some people are more aware of this emptiness than are others. It can show up in a preference to be constantly busy so you don't have the time to reflect on your feelings. Or, you may numb your awareness by drinking too much alcohol or taking drugs. You might notice that you become irritated when asked about your deeper feelings. Avoidance of this awareness is frequently a sign that there is something missing; something you would prefer to ignore because you have no clue as to how to fill it.

TASK: See if you can get in touch with this inner emptiness. Make a list of questions you prefer to ignore about your life. See if you can discover a deep longing from something more than you have in your life.

EXERCISE 4C – SPIRITUALITY, ERODING

Exercise 4 invites you to notice that when you have insufficient spirituality you don't experience the success you expect. Your life is eroding despite your efforts. You may or may not understand why it is declining or what you can do to arrest the downward slide. Spirituality not only contributes a sense of meaning and purpose, it also provides a framework of values that support material success. Attributes like diligence, self-discipline, and zeal lead to productivity and responsibility. Without sufficient spirituality you may lack values such as these and so lack the ability to consistently be productive.

TASK: Review the areas of your life that are in decline. See if you can list of values that you might be missing.

SESSION 4

EXERCISE 1D – SPIRITUALITY, ERODING

Session 4 focuses your attention on ways you can cultivate greater spiritual awareness. Let's get started.

Exercise 1 invites you to ask yourself big questions. If you pay attention, you may notice that much conversation is about trivial things. People talk about the weather. News reports on local crime and political wrangling. Rarely, does conversation involve deeper, life-changing, and soul-provoking questions. "What is the meaning of life?" "What happens when you die?" "What is the most satisfying way to live?" These are not easy questions to answer. In fact, they may not have definitive answers. But, considering such questions deepens your understanding and appreciation of life. All of these questions are important. Any insights you have about them may change how you live your life.

TASK: Make a list of questions such as these that you will ask yourself on a daily basis. Set aside 15 minutes each day to consider them.

EXERCISE 2D – SPIRITUALITY, ERODING

Exercise 2 invites you to practice meditation. There are many forms of meditation and all of them are useful. Perhaps the simplest is to sit in a chair, close your eyes, and breathe deeply. Meditation will slow you down and unclutter your mind so you can better access deeper parts of your mind and heart. As you become more comfortable with meditation, you might find yourself becoming more centered and focused in your everyday life. You can cultivate a depth that was lacking. Silence is very important in cultivating spirituality. The more you silence your active mind, the more open you are to hear new things.

TASK: Practice meditation each day for 15 minutes.

EXERCISE 3D – SPIRITUALITY, ERODING

Exercise 3 invites you to practice meditating about your death. Death is a profound topic because it is an event we all will experience and over which we have no control. It is a game changer to say the least. Many people avoid thinking about their death as if by ignoring it, somehow it will go away. Meditating about your death is a way of embracing its truth so you can live your life in a new way. Each day becomes precious when you live in the context of your death. Close your eyes and pick a place where you imagine your death. Focus on what it will be like when you are facing the last five minutes of your life. After a few minutes, focus on the last minute of your life. Then, focus on the last thirty seconds. Then the last five seconds. Finally, the very last second.

TASK: Practice this at least once each week.

EXERCISE 4D – SPIRITUALITY, ERODING

Exercise 4 invites you to cultivate goodness. Goodness is a spiritual quality that is easy to expand by practice. Every day provides ample opportunity to demonstrate goodness.

TASK: You can choose to hold the door for a stranger. You can pay the check for someone in a restaurant. You can smile at someone you don't know. Practice expanding how you show goodness to your family and friends. Take coffee to your partner in the morning. Take extra time to play with your children. Be conscious of new opportunities to practice goodness. Notice how it changes you and your life.

FACTOR – SPIRITUALITY

While we are not preaching any theology, we are advocating that spirituality is a necessary component to finding your true purpose. Spirituality simply acknowledges that the Universe is bigger than you.

SELF-ASSESSED RATING - TREADING WATER

You experience spirituality and value it in your life but don't consciously cultivate it, and so miss much of its power to expand your life.

SESSION 1

EXERCISE 1A – SPIRITUALITY, TREADING WATER

You are treading water, at least partly, because of the state of your spirituality. You must have some understanding of spirituality even if you are not fully aware; otherwise, your life would not be as functional as it is. Session 1 focuses your attention on a better understanding of what spirituality is. Let's get started.

Exercise 1 invites you to see that spirituality is seeing a bigger picture. There are things you know, right? Then, there are things you know you don't know. You may know that you don't know how to speak German. There are many things you know you don't know. Then, there are the things you don't know you know. That is a lot of things. That being the case, you know so little of what there is to know, yet every day you make critical decisions that impact your life. Who would buy a car based only on a color or buy a house without knowing how many rooms it had? Spirituality is the quest to know more. If you come across as someone who has all of the answers, you aren't demonstrating much spirituality. If you are curious and always asking yourself bigger questions, you are demonstrating spirituality.

TASK: Rate your curiosity and openness from 1 (not open at all) to 5 (extremely open).

EXERCISE 2A – SPIRITUALITY, TREADING WATER

Exercise 2 invites you to see that spirituality is an interest in goodness in all of its forms. True spirituality is the desire to see good in yourself and in others, and to expand that goodness wherever you can. Spirituality doesn't lead to selfishness, meanness, bitterness, or resentment. Instead, it seeks that which is good for others and that which supports kindness, collaboration, and peace. Notice how much you value goodness. It may be easy for you to identify goodness in your love for your family. You likely act in their best interest even when it is costly. One of the gifts in raising children is the challenge to expand your goodness. It is for goodness sake that you soothe frightened and crying children in the middle of the night, putting their comfort ahead of your sleep.

TASK: Rate your interest in supporting goodness from 1 (very high) to 5 (quite low).

EXERCISE 3A – SPIRITUALITY, TREADING WATER

Exercise 3 invites you to see that spirituality is the desire for transformation. When you are committed to being spiritual, you see the need for continual growth and change. You have a deep desire to become less material and more spiritual. You are willing to let go of habits and desires that interfere with that growth and to acquire habits that support it. You are willing to be changed and to be different even when others don't understand or connect with your evolving spirituality.

TASK: See if you can see evidence that you have been involved in being transformed. Rate your level of transformation from 1 (profound) to 5 (slight, if any).

EXERCISE 4A – SPIRITUALITY, TREADING WATER

Exercise 4 invites you to see that spirituality is a sensitive and active conscience. When you are spiritual, you tend to monitor your thoughts, attitudes, and behaviors. You feel badly when you are petty or create harm. You learn from those mistakes and change in ways that reduce the likelihood that such things will occur again. You apologize to those you have hurt, and do what you can to make amends. When you lack spirituality, you pay little attention to the consequences of your choices, and care little about how others are impacted. You are rarely sorry and do little to repair any damage you may have created.

TASK: Rate the sensitivity of your conscience from 1 (quite sensitive) to 5 (not sensitive at all).

SESSION 2

EXERCISE 1B – SPIRITUALITY, TREADING WATER

Session 2 focuses your attention on some of the benefits you are receiving because of your spirituality. You may or may not be aware of how much your spirituality is contributing to the health and goodness of your life. Let's get started.

Exercise 1 invites you to see that your spirituality makes you an attractive person. We are not referring to your physical attractiveness, but that of your being. You are the kind of person that people enjoy being around, want on their team, and seek out as a friend. You carry yourself with a decency and goodness that people sense. You can open your eyes to these qualities by simply noticing that people like you and seek your company, and then asking yourself what people find to be attractive. It is important that you see what they see.

TASK: Every day this week notice how people treat you. When they show interest and preference for you, see if you can figure out why. Make a list of those qualities.

EXERCISE 2B – SPIRITUALITY, TREADING WATER

Exercise 2 invites you to see that your spirituality gives you a big perspective on your life. You tend to think about where you are headed and how you will get there. There is a planfulness and order to your life that others don't share. Seeing your life in the context of a bigger plan allows you to prioritize activities and events based on their contribution to your overall plan. Hence, you tend to make wise decisions and avoid problems that those who are less spiritual fall into. It is important that you notice your natural inclination to view your life from a big perspective, and the benefits you have derived from doing so.

TASK: Write down the goal for your life and then list some of the good decisions you have made as a result of your perspective.

EXERCISE 3B – SPIRITUALITY, TREADING WATER

Exercise 3 invites you to see that your spirituality provides you with a strong moral compass. You have a sense of right and wrong that guides your thoughts and behavior. It isn't that you always do what is right and avoid doing what is wrong. But, as a compass allows you to successfully chart a course, your values help you to successfully navigate life. You are thoughtful about the things you choose to do and not do. You have the ability to evaluate what is truly in your best interest and the things you should avoid. As a result, you have fewer regrets than do those who are less spiritual. Many things work out for you in a natural and easeful way.

TASK: Write down at least five of the values that guide your life. Next, list some decisions those values have helped you to make.

EXERCISE 4B – SPIRITUALITY, TREADING WATER

Exercise 4 invites you to see that your spirituality provides you with a win/win mentality. You don't live your life as if it is you against the world. You experience a sense of connectedness to people, to nature, and to life itself that prompts you to think about the good of the whole. You trust that if you do the right thing, things will work out pretty well for you. Hence, your choices and decisions tend to work out well for the people around you as well as for yourself. People like working for you. They like having you on their team. They like being your friend. They find that good things happen when you are involved. You exude a positive energy that attracts positivity from others and from life.

TASK: See if you can list five examples of your win/win attitude. List at least two benefits that have come from each of those examples.

SESSION 3

EXERCISE 1C – SPIRITUALITY, TREADING WATER

Session 3 focuses your attention on some of the limitations of your spirituality, and how those limitations might be holding you back from growing. Despite your awareness of a force bigger than you, you still struggle to trust fully that you can rely on that power to provide and care for you. You continue to demonstrate a fair amount of willfulness. Let's get started.

Exercise 1 invites you to notice that while sometimes you see the big picture, often you don't trust life. You might like to believe in the goodness of life toward you but there are times when you don't see it that way. You have limits to your faith in goodness. And, when you are frightened and lacking trust you lose track of the benefit of your spirituality. In fact, you run counter to it.

TASK: See if you can identify times and/or circumstances when you haven't trusted the goodness of life. Notice if there are particular issues that cause you to lose faith.

EXERCISE 2C – SPIRITUALITY, TREADING WATER

Exercise 2 invites you to see that when you lose trust in the goodness of life you seize control and begin driving things. You may notice this as an abrupt transition or as a subtle change. You are relaxed and open, and then a thought comes into your mind that generates anxiety. Rather than noticing and wondering what this is about, you leap into action trying to force things as you think they should go. Because your actions are motivated by fear and not connected to your spiritual perspective, they don't work as well as you wish causing you to redouble your effort. This could happen at work when you have taken on an important project and lose trust that it will work out. It can also happen at home when there is a problem or an accident, and you suddenly take over in an effort to regain a sense of control.

TASK: Make a list of five times when your loss of trust resulted in your taking control and trying to make things happen.

EXERCISE 3C – SPIRITUALITY, TREADING WATER

Exercise 3 invites you to see that your loss of trust and seizing of control brings with it excessive worry. When you are not in touch with your spirituality you find yourself full of worry. Your worry might start small but it can quickly escalate. The thought that you could be laid off mushrooms into anxiety about losing your house and living with your family on the street. Worry about getting sick becomes a preoccupation with having cancer and dying. Worry is a clear sign that you are taking responsibility for things you cannot control, and have lost your ability to center yourself in the goodness of life.

TASK: Notice how much time you spend worrying and the things you tend to worry about. Worry will show you the limits of your spirituality and the aspects of your life over which you can begin to surrender control.

EXERCISE 4C – SPIRITUALITY, TREADING WATER

Exercise 4 invites you to see that when you lose track of your spirituality and begin treating your life as if it happens by your effort and will, you end up depleting and exhausting yourself. Life is so much bigger than you. The effort to bend it to fit your wishes is all-consuming because life can't be bent by you. It is impossible to secure yourself in the world. The illusion that money can make you feel safe quickly vanishes when you have money and realize you still don't feel safe. You know that money can't protect you from accidents and illness.

TASK: Make a list of times when you have gotten out of balance and exhausted yourself because you had wandered away from your spirituality, and were burdening yourself with issues you could not solve.

SESSION 4

EXERCISE 1D – SPIRITUALITY, TREADING WATER

Session 4 focuses your attention on ways you can expand your spirituality so you can move from treading water to growing. Let's get started.

Exercise 1 invites you to learn to surrender. In Session 3 you learned that taking control is one reaction to losing trust. Another is to surrender. Surrender is an act of faith. When you make this choice you don't take action. Instead, you quiet your heart and be still. Surrender is a practice that will expand your spirituality. You can practice surrender whenever you feel the temptation to rally your energy and effort because you are frightened about something that is happening. Your child is sick and you are scared. You can call everyone you know and bother the doctors and nurses every minute. Or you quiet yourself and be present to the moment. It is in the quiet that you will find both strength and peace.

TASK: Practice being still in the presence of forces bigger that yourself. You may sit on your porch in a raging summer storm and quiet yourself. You may sit on the beach and make yourself quiet in the presence of massive surf.

EXERCISE 2D – SPIRITUALITY, TREADING WATER

Exercise 2 invites you to practice trust. Now that you have learned to quiet yourself, you can cultivate expanding your trust. But, trust in what? Not trust that you will always get the outcome you want. That misplaced trust will lead you to disappointment, bitterness, and the loss of your spirituality. Instead, you can cultivate trust in the goodness of life that, if you choose to believe it, is vaster that you can imagine. You may not get what you asked for, but in its place you may receive something far bigger and more satisfying. To put yourself in such a frame of mind and heart, you must trust.

TASK: Practice trusting the goodness of life by noticing when you become attached to something you want, and then imagine something even better that might make your desire seem petty and empty.

EXERCISE 3D – SPIRITUALITY, TREADING WATER

Exercise 3 invites you to practice acceptance. Acceptance will push your trust still deeper. Acceptance requires giving up resistance to whatever happens. How do you know how things should turn out? How do you know how you should be treated? Why do you think you should have pleasure but not pain, or joy but now sorrow? Have you determined that one is good and the other is bad? Acceptance gives up such categories and receives whatever life sends as you might accept the sunshine and the rain. Neither is good or bad. They are just different. When you are treated well, accept it. When you are mistreated and hurt, accept it. Learn to live from a place of fundamental acceptance for whatever occurs. Acceptance will expand your spirituality.

TASK: Notice what you might be resisting in this moment. Write it down. Now, practice accepting it.

EXERCISE 4D – SPIRITUALITY, TREADING WATER

Exercise 4 invites you to cultivate the practice of wonder. Wonder is a foundational practice in cultivating spirituality because wonder acknowledges that we know so little and have so much to learn. When you wonder, you invite life to be your teacher, mentor, and guide. There is so much about which you can wonder. You can wonder about the purpose of life and how you can connect with it. You can wonder about the source of beauty and goodness. You can wonder what lesson is embedded in everything that will occur today, and how many of those lessons you are prepared to receive. You can wonder how you can be more loving and good. You can wonder how the Universe works. You can wonder about the mystery of life. These are very big issues. The more you consider them, the greater you expand yourself and your ability to see with spiritual eyes.

TASK: Set aside at least 15 minutes each day just to wonder.

FACTOR – SPIRITUALITY

While we are not preaching any theology, we are advocating that spirituality is a necessary component to finding your true purpose. Spirituality simply acknowledges that the Universe is bigger than you.

SELF-ASSESSED RATING - GROWING

You understand and cultivate spirituality through practices that expand its influence into most parts of your life.

SESSION 1

EXERCISE 1A – SPIRITUALITY, GROWING

Your life is growing, at least partly, because you have a well-developed spirituality. The goal of these exercises is to help you to better understand the concept of spirituality, how it contributes to the strength of your life, and ways you can continue to grow and develop in this area. Session 1 focuses your attention on various aspects of spirituality. Let's get started.

Exercise 1 invites you to recognize that spirituality is an acknowledgement of a force or presence that is foundational to everything. This is a very big idea because the existence of such a presence must become the most important factor in organizing everything in your life. What could be more important than better understanding the nature of such a force and how to effectively relate to it? How you define yourself, how you live your life, and what you make important is all determined by this reality.

TASK: Take a few minutes to reflect on how much you organize your life around this acknowledgement. Rate yourself from 1 (organize everything around it) to 5 (organize very little around it).

EXERCISE 2A – SPIRITUALITY, GROWING

Exercise 2 invites you to see that spirituality radically determines your character. Those who have a well-developed spirituality have well-defined and deeply embraced values that form how they think and do every day and in every circumstance. In other words, spirituality is not only ideas which people believe, but it becomes a way of living. Spirituality provides an owner's manual for life. It tells you how life is meant to be lived and how it is cared for. Those who embrace spirituality live by that manual and shape their lives according to it.

TASK: Rate how much your character is shaped by your spirituality from 1 (Everything is constantly shaped by it) to 5 (Hardly anything is shaped by it).

EXERCISE 3A – SPIRITUALITY, GROWING

Exercise 3 invites you to see that spiritualty creates a unique relationship to the world. Those who are spiritual relate to the world as if they are intimately connected to everything and everyone. They see themselves as a manifestation of the same "life" that every living thing possesses, and hence responsible to care for and respect life in all of its forms. Spirituality manifests itself in such qualities as love, honor, fairness, generosity, responsibility, and goodness. Hence, those who are spiritual demonstrate this very special relationship to the world in all that they do. Their interest in their welfare becomes secondary to their interest in the welfare of the whole.

TASK: Rate your relationship to the world from 1 (completely guided by my spirituality) to 5 (not at all guided by my spirituality).

EXERCISE 4A – SPIRITUALITY, GROWING

Exercise 4 invites you to see that spirituality has an aspirational quality to it. You might say that the force of spirituality is always creating, refining, and improving. Evolution is a constant process of adaptation and changes that result in innovation and progress. Those who are spiritual are committed to the constant and continual cultivation of their spiritual character; letting go of what impedes it and embracing practices, disciplines, and habits that develop it. It is as if spirituality is in the process of making life deeper, richer, and better and those who are spiritual are committed to being an integral part of that process.

TASK: Rate your life in terms of your spiritual aspiration from 1 (very motivated to grow in spirituality) to 5 (not motivated at all to grow in spirituality).

SESSION 2

EXERCISE 1B – SPIRITUALITY, GROWING

Session 2 focuses your attention on some of the ways your spirituality has supported your success in life. Seeing its value will encourage you to continue to expand it. Let's get started.

Exercise 1 invites you to see that your spirituality contributes greater toward making you a high- quality person. You are the kind of person that people admire and try to emulate. You have your act together and it is obvious to everyone. Your life seems to be both rich and deep, but in ways that people don't understand. You seem free from the rat race that fills the lives of so many people. You don't seem all that attached to your possessions, as if you can enjoy them but not need them. Your life is an example of what life can be for everyone if they are willing to cultivate spirituality.

TASK: List five things about you and your life that you can see others admire. See if you can identify how they are rooted in your spirituality.

EXERCISE 2B – SPIRITUALITY, GROWING

Exercise 2 invites you to see that your spirituality provides you with real meaning and purpose for your life. You see so many people who have their heads down and are working hard but without awareness of where they are going or why they want to get there. They are working to be wealthy but are exhausting themselves and burning out the important relationships in their life in that pursuit. They are hoping to create security but you can see that their plan cannot provide it. You, on the other hand, can clearly see how your life makes a difference in the world around you. You understand how being yourself fits into your world and makes a significant contribution. As a result, you work with determination but also with balance. You feel secure regardless of your wealth or position. You have a sense of significance even when you aren't being recognized by those around you.

TASK: List five ways you feel your life is meaningful and purposeful. Now, list five of the benefits you get from having such a clear sense of purpose.

EXERCISE 3B – SPIRITUALITY, GROWING

Exercise 3 invites you to see that your spirituality provides you with the strength and conviction to hold your course even when things are difficult and demanding. You certainly enjoy life when you are succeeding and things are going well. But, when times become difficult, you don't panic and abandon your plan. You seem to have an inner confidence that if you stay on course everything will work out in the end. That confidence allows you to be strong in your conviction and steady in your actions. Your steadiness pays off as you keep building on the foundation you established. People can see the progress that results from your ability to be resolute and to persevere in hardship.

TASK: List five times when you can see your ability to be strong and to persevere when things were difficult.

EXERCISE 4B – SPIRITUALITY, GROWING

Exercise 4 invites you to see that your spirituality causes you to shine in the world. This is not a benefit that is easy to put in to words. But, as you grow in your spirituality your life more and more radiates spirit. Just as the sun radiates light, you radiate goodness, belief, honor, kindness, beauty, compassion, patience, and joy. You become a person who naturally invites others into a spiritual journey. People are attracted to you for the right reasons; they sense something about you that feels eternal and limitless. This quality about you is your source of leadership. You gather people to expand goodness, to bring healing and mercy, and to continue in the transformation of the world in goodness.

TASK: See if you can list five ways you see yourself shining in the world. Notice in particular how you impact the people you meet.

SESSION 3

EXERCISE 1C – SPIRITUALITY, GROWING

Session 3 focuses your attention on some limitations to your spirituality that may be holding you back from fully thriving. These are areas for growth. Let's get started.

Exercise 1 invites you to see that despite your growth in spirituality your smallness never completely goes away. Even though you radiate spirit, the temptations of life surround you. You see others measuring themselves by external things such as their wealth, the size of their home, and how expensively they dress and you find yourself wanting to compete. You have lapses when you use your spiritual power for selfish ends. You sometimes forget the big picture and become petty, reactionary, negative, and judgmental. You have been to high places in your spiritual journey but find that, on occasion, it is as if you never started along the spiritual path.

TASK: Make a list of at least five times when you have strayed from your spiritual journey and acted in a small and petty way.

EXERCISE 2C – SPIRITUALITY, GROWING

Exercise 2 invites you to see that despite your trust in the goodness of life, sometimes you doubt. Occasionally, your doubt is so big as to question the very existence of the spiritual realm. Normally, though, you find yourself doubting your commitment, your ability to follow the path and the benefits of being true to your spiritual journey. Doubt limits your ability to fully give yourself to your spiritual experience and to be consistently filled up with all that it has to offer you. Doubt shows up most fully when you encounter difficulty and suffering.

TASK: List at least five times when you found yourself doubting.

EXERCISE 3C – SPIRITUALITY, GROWING

Exercise 3 invites you to see that despite your spirituality, sometimes you are frightened and anxious. You know anxiety is the result of becoming committed to some outcome you don't control, but you can't help yourself. From time to time you allow some things to become more important than your commitment to live a spirit-filled life. Such things can sneak up on you. You value your marriage and want it to last a lifetime. You love your children and don't want anything to hurt them. You like living in your house and want to keep it forever. When those things are threatened, you get scared. You stop trusting and grab the steering wheel in the hope that you can make things turn out as you wish. You don't see that your effort is pointless and that you have lost connection with the source of your joy and peace.

TASK: List at least five times when you tried to take over control of your life because you were scared.

EXERCISE 4C – SPIRITUALITY, GROWING

Exercise 4 invites you to see that despite your spirituality, sometimes you hold back. You can feel the calling of spirituality to grow, but you also know that spiritual growth comes at a price. You will need to surrender some comforts and habits because they get in the way of your spiritual development. You will need to take on some new challenges, to show up in new ways, and to accept being increasingly different from your friends and family who have no interest in the world of spirit. At times, this journey seems too much for you and you get to a point where you are unwilling to move forward. Your spiritual growth slows and languishes. Perhaps you are in such a place right now. You have been growing in some ways but not in others. You know you need to get back on track if you are to thrive.

TASK: Make a list of things you need to change to get fully on your spiritual journey. See if you are willing to make those changes.

SESSION 4

EXERCISE 1D – SPIRITUALITY, GROWING

Session 4 focuses on some specific practices you can begin that can assist you in further developing your spirituality. Let's get started.

Exercise 1 invites you to take on the practice of being quiet. In order to be quiet you must slow down, sit still, empty your busy mind, stop talking, and listen. When you learn to listen well, you tune into the world of spirit. There are ways of knowing that are much deeper than traditional teaching of the mind through education. There is a deeper knowing of the heart and the soul that is only accomplished through quiet.

TASK: Practice being quiet at least three times each day. Occasionally, practice being quiet when others are talking. Notice what you hear when you are being quiet.

EXERCISE 2D – SPIRITUALITY, GROWING

Exercise 2 invites you to take on the practice of rituals that support your spirituality. Rituals are simply behaviors that you consistently perform. Everyone has rituals. Brushing your teeth is likely to be one. Rituals that support spiritual development are behaviors that you consciously choose to do because they remind you of the world of spirit or directly connect you to it. Exercises 3 and 4 will outline two specific rituals, but you are free to choose your own. For some, attending a religious service is a ritual. Reading spiritual material can be a ritual. Meditation can become a ritual. The best way to form your rituals is to notice those things you do that most cultivate your spiritual development.

TASK: Once you have identified them, make a conscious decision about when, where, and how often you will engage in those activities. Then, stick with the routine. The regularity of rituals is a large part of their benefit.

EXERCISE 3D – SPIRITUALITY, GROWING

Exercise 3 invites you to consider taking on the ritual of regular prayer. Prayer is many things to many people. Some people say a prayer of thanks before they eat, or say a prayer at the end of their day as they retire. Most importantly, prayer is a time to focus only on the world of spirit and to connect to it as directly as you can. Prayer is often more about listening than about speaking, allowing your thoughts, feelings, reactions and desires to be shaped by your spirituality. Prayer can be a time when you seek to be directed in your decisions by your spirituality. The ritual of prayer can be a powerful way of more completely aligning yourself with the world of spirit.

TASK: Cultivate a habit of prayer by deciding when, where, and how often you will pray. Then, engage in prayer however it suits you according to your schedule.

EXERCISE 4D – SPIRITUALITY, GROWING

Exercise 4 invites you to consider taking on the ritual of sacrifice. This might sound worse than it is. Most religions have well prescribed rituals of sacrifice. Some include fasting; times when you either go without eating or eat very little. Others have times of the year when you give up some indulgence, or days when you don't eat certain foods. The benefit of the ritual of sacrifice is to get yourself used to giving up attachments for a higher, spiritual end. It is training in attaching your desires and wishes to the world of spirit. You should decide how you would like to practice sacrifice. One way to do so is by charitable giving. You give away some of your money to those who have greater needs. There is great benefit to you when you practice sacrificing the money you earned.

TASK: Pick one or two ways you would like to practice sacrifice and make them rituals.

Manufactured by Amazon.ca
Bolton, ON

32753774R00136